Raising Rosie

of related interest

He's Always Been My Son
A Mother's Story about
Raising Her Transgender Son
Janna Barkin
ISBN 978 1 78592 747 8
eISBN 978 1 78450 525 7

The Gender Agenda
A First-Hand Account of How Girls
and Boys Are Treated Differently
Ros Ball and James Millar
Foreword by Marianne Grabrucker
ISBN 978 1 78592 320 3
eISBN 978 1 78450 633 9

Straight Expectations
The Story of a Family in Transition
Peggy Cryden, LMFT
ISBN 978 1 78592 748 5
eISBN 978 1 78450 537 0

Becoming an Ally to the
Gender-Expansive Child
A Guide for Parents and Carers
Anna Bianchi
ISBN 978 1 78592 051 6
eISBN 978 1 78450 305 5

Raising Rosie

Our Story of Parenting an Intersex Child

Eric Lohman and Stephani Lohman
Foreword by Georgiann Davis

Jessica Kingsley *Publishers*
London and Philadelphia

First published in 2018
by Jessica Kingsley Publishers
73 Collier Street
London N1 9BE, UK
and
400 Market Street, Suite 400
Philadelphia, PA 19106, USA

www.jkp.com

Library of Congress Cataloging in Publication Data
A CIP catalog record for this book is available from the Library of Congress

British Library Cataloguing in Publication Data
A CIP catalogue record for this book is available from the British Library

ISBN 978 1 78592 767 6
eISBN 978 1 78450 652 0

Printed and bound in the United States

CONTENTS

FOREWORD

Georgiann Davis

It was in the early 1990s when an older, balding, Greek immigrant doctor with glasses as thick as his accent told my mother and me that I would never be able to have biological children. I wasn't fazed. I was thirteen years old and wanted another dog, not a baby! However, my mother, a Greek immigrant herself, was devastated. More than twenty years have passed and I can still hear her sobbing. Only now I know that the source of her uncontrollable tears was that she was privately told the truth about my body which I was not: I'm intersex. The doctor made her feel horrible when he framed my body as a medical abnormality that needed to be surgically fixed—feelings that were exasperated when he instructed both of my parents to never tell me the truth about my body. With this medical advice that my parents followed, my doctor, and his colleagues, constructed a ball of shame and secrecy that my entire family would have to spend years unraveling.

I was born in October of 1980 with an external female appearance, but inside, instead of XX chromosomes, ovaries, a uterus, and fallopian tubes, I have XY chromosomes and testes; that is, I *had* testes before a surgeon removed them because, in his limited mindset, a girl couldn't have balls. I wouldn't learn the truth about my body until years later when I privately obtained my medical records. As I read through the redacted text that outlined my intersex diagnosis (Complete Androgen Insensitivity Syndrome) and also communicated the doctors' problematic justifications for why they felt it was best to lie to me and tell me I had ovarian cancer rather than explain that I was intersex, I felt like a freak and I was angry. While I don't agree with them, I understand that doctors were worried the development of my gender identity would be disrupted if I knew I was intersex. However, I'm still shocked they thought lying to me and telling me I had cancer would somehow be better. I've since dedicated my life to fighting for the human rights of intersex people as both an activist and a feminist medical sociologist.

Words can't quite articulate what it feels like to know Stephani and Eric Lohman, parents who have been intersex advocates from the very beginning of their intersex child's life. But, I will try. As they courageously continue to challenge medical authority, negotiate complicated privacy issues, and collaboratively join intersex activists in the fight for intersex human rights, they always center Rosie—their beautiful intersex child. If *Raising Rosie* is an indication of how at least some of today's parents of intersex children are navigating their child's intersex diagnosis, I'm confident I might just live to see an end to the medically unnecessary and irreversible interventions designed to erase rather than embrace intersex.

Of course, the Lohmans aren't raising Rosie alone. As they describe in the pages that follow, they are standing on the shoulders of many intersex activists from around the world. The global intersex rights movement was formed in the late 1980s and early 1990s, and since, it has grown in size and power. The first wave of intersex activists successfully raised intersex visibility and awareness about the horrific medical practices intersex people were routinely forced to endure without their consent. Doctors can no longer claim ignorance, as they certainly know intersex people are angry about intersex medicalization practices. Yet, doctors continue to perform so-called "normalization" surgeries on intersex bodies that deprive youths of their bodily autonomy. I want to make very clear that, like the Lohmans, I am not against intersex surgical interventions. Instead, I only ask that the intersex person themselves choose what, if any, medical interventions they receive. This is not an unreasonable request.

I trust *Raising Rose* will positively impact society, especially other parents of intersex children, in countless ways for years to come. But, with that said, I still want to publicly and preemptively reflect on the issue of Rosie's privacy that may surface during your reading of *Raising Rosie*. What does it mean that Rosie's parents have publicly shared their family's story? I read courage. I feel love. I see advocacy. And, most importantly, I accept *Raising Rosie* as evidence that we, people personally connected to intersex, can indeed dismantle the thin and blurry line between privacy and shame. Intersex is not shameful. It doesn't need to be hidden from the world any more than a child's birthday, school report card, winning soccer goal, or college admission decision does. I caution all of us personally connected to intersex to think about what we, consciously or not, perpetuate when we forcefully sandwich "privacy" and "intersex" in the same concern. By fixating on privacy concerns, are we unintentionally fueling the same intersex struggles we are trying to wrestle?

In my sociological research on intersex in contemporary U.S. society, I advocate that parents of intersex children need not only medical information about intersex before they consent to any irreversible medical interventions, but also, more importantly, they must receive a different kind of information—information that comes from being connected with the intersex community. Parents need to know they aren't alone. They need to know that intersex is a natural sex variation. They need to know that their intersex child will love and be loved and that their child's intersex trait will not restrict the dreams they have for their child. *Raising Rosie* is an excellent resource for those wishing to engage with a different kind of information. Stephani and Eric vulnerably share their earliest concerns when Rosie was born, outline their decision-making process that led them to refuse problematic cosmetic surgeries, describe their advocacy efforts, and in the process, they offer recommendations for other parents of intersex children, medical professionals, and policy makers.

When I publicly speak about intersex, I'm often asked if I harbor any disappointment or resentment towards my parents for consenting to medically unnecessary interventions on my body, while simultaneously lying to me about my intersex diagnosis. While I understand the question, it often confuses me. My parents were simply following the advice of medical professionals. They would never want to physically or emotionally harm me. As I argue throughout my scholarship, parents of intersex children are pawns in the medicalization process. They are rarely told that intersex is a natural bodily variation. Instead, intersex is often presented to them as a medical problem that should be medically corrected. In these ways, the parents of intersex children are also forced to navigate problematic intersex medicalization practices. And my parents, like the Lohmans, are no exception.

My parents have never met other parents of intersex children. And given they are both terminally ill, I do not know if they ever will. But I know they are comforted by the fact that parent advocates like the Lohmans exist so that future parents of intersex children will not have to endure what our family did.

Raising Rosie is an inspirational account of our community's ongoing fight for intersex human rights. I hope you are as moved by it as I am.

Georgiann Davis, PhD, is an intersex scholar and activist originally from Chicago, Illinois. She joined the University of Nevada, Las Vegas' Sociology Department in the fall of 2014 after spending close to ten years studying the intersection of the sociology of diagnosis and feminist theories. In her book, Contesting Intersex: The Dubious Diagnosis

(2015, NYU Press), Davis explores how intersex is defined, experienced, and contested in contemporary U.S. society. She is also the board president of interACT: Advocates for Intersex Youth (2017 to present) and the former president of the AIS-DSD Support Group (2014 to 2015). You can read more about her work at www.georgianndavis.com.

To all the brave intersex activists, whose courage and resilience continue to inspire us.

And to Rosie, who has the freedom to live the life she wants, thanks to so many brave intersex people who came before her.

INTRODUCTION

Together we have raised four children and, with every pregnancy, the first question that we got was always regarding the child's gender assignment. "Is it a boy, or a girl?" they would ask. Or, "Do you hope it's a girl, or boy?" This is a standard line of questioning for anyone expecting a baby. Before we, as a society, can begin to make sense of that child as a tiny human, we must first know what the gender is. It allows us to start making assumptions about their future, to connect with the parents, to begin making sense of the child as someone who will one day have a personality, desires, and goals. For many of us, we must first know the gender if we're to know what gifts to buy, and what colors to associate with him or her. Everything that follows depends on stability in this first category. This is perhaps why, when a child presents with ambiguous physical markers of gender, it is considered a medical emergency, and sets in motion a series of actions that have led to irreparable damage to the lives of innocent people. This is what happened to us when in 2012 we delivered Rosie, who is intersex, but has had no surgeries. At the time of writing this, she is a happy, healthy five-year-old. Rosie is our youngest child. By the time she was born, we were no strangers to the questions from people about the expected gender of our child. This is why, when the ultrasound revealed that our baby was going to be a girl, we relayed that to people who asked, and began planning for a girl. When that baby girl arrived, and doctors saw that her body was not what they expected, things went from exciting to scary in a matter of seconds.

Suddenly, we found ourselves thrust into a situation for which we were not entirely prepared. Our daughter was diagnosed with a rare and serious genetic condition called Congenital Adrenal Hyperplasia (or CAH) which can cause girls to be born with ambiguous genitalia. Her health was not only in jeopardy, but our small family was located in Canada at the time, while our extended family network was still in the United States, so we found ourselves without the safety net to which we were accustomed. We were navigating a healthcare system that was unfamiliar to us, and trying to maintain some level of normalcy in our daily family routine, while struggling to make sense of our baby's condition, which kept her in the neonatal intensive care unit for three weeks. I was doing graduate work, Stephani was planning to start nursing school, and suddenly everything ground to a halt while we tried to process this unexpected turn of events. All that aside, perhaps our biggest obstacle came from the pediatric urological surgeon, who pressured us relentlessly over the next few months to consent to a "normalizing" cosmetic procedure on our child's genitalia.

The surgeon was not the only source of pressure to consent to a surgery. We quickly found that parent and advocacy groups associated with our child's specific condition were deficient sources of information on raising a surgery-free intersex child. This is partly due, we suspect, to the fact that several prominent pediatric urological surgeons are affiliated directly with CAH groups such as the CARES Foundation. The general impression we got from these organizations was that, if we wanted to avoid surgery they supported that choice, so long as we kept that decision to ourselves. We were unable to find any other parents on social media or otherwise that had children born with similar conditions who had opted against a cosmetic genital procedure in infancy (we have since found fewer than ten families, almost all of whom choose to remain discreet about their decision). The more objective and critical resources that we did find, and which are shared in this book, made a very convincing case for why we should not consent to surgery, but even this material is not very helpful in discussing ways for new parents to raise an intersex child.

We could not understand why the argument for delaying surgery was not more widely accepted by CAH parent groups. Why did we have to dig so deep to find this information? It is our hope that this book can serve as a guide for new parents of intersex children, which can help you make a decision that you feel assured is in the best interest of your child, as well as provide strategies for dealing with the unique challenges of raising a healthy and happy intersex youth. If you are considering surgery for your intersex child, or if you are facing pressure to consent to surgery, or if you have made up your mind against surgery and want to know what to do next, this book is for you.

But this book is not only for parents of intersex children. There are many critical stakeholders who may be in a position to influence policy on how we treat intersex children socially, culturally, legally, politically, and medically. If you are reading this, it is possible that you are one of these stakeholders, and you perhaps find yourself, like us when Rosie was born, wholly unprepared to meet the challenges you now face. Nurses, teachers, politicians and grandparents all have a critical role to play in ensuring that the treatment of intersex kids is fair and just. You may not have an intersex child of your own, but if you work at a hospital you may be able to do something about policies on cosmetic genital surgery. You may not have an intersex child in your family, but if you are a politician you can sponsor legislation that supports the rights of these children to bodily autonomy and informed consent. You may not know an intersex child, but if you are a teacher you can make sure that any intersex children that come to your school are made to feel safe, welcome, and respected.

Medicalization of intersex conditions

Many people do not understand what it means to be intersex, but the term is not that complicated, really. It is an umbrella term that describes people who are born with a variety of physical characteristics that do not fit neatly into traditional ideas about male and female bodies. This encompasses things like genital variation, such as ambiguous genitalia (an enlarged clitoris, or a micro-penis). Intersex can also refer to genetic ambiguity, like children born with XXY chromosomes, or organ variations including the presence of undescended testes in the abdomen of a woman. In other cases, it can refer to atypical hormonal levels, like hyperandrogenism (high levels of testosterone in women). Whether or not these conditions present any serious medical problems is dependent on a host of factors, and varies from person to person. Intersex conditions can be very contentious because, while medical tests may objectively diagnose a person as having one condition or another, whether an individual identifies as intersex is completely subjective. For example, while Rosie has ambiguous genitalia, widely accepted as an intersex trait, as a result of having CAH, some women with CAH who were also born with ambiguous genitalia do not identify as intersex. We respect the rights of people to identify in ways they feel most comfortable but, as we will discuss in later chapters, we feel that raising Rosie as an intersex person preserves her ability to decide for herself how she feels most comfortable identifying as she grows older, and also places her in the inclusive group of people with bodies like hers, a safe, welcoming space. Surgical alterations to her body without her input, we feel, would contradict that goal.

Variations in our bodies like this seem to challenge our traditional conceptions of gender and sexuality. However, the reality is that intersex conditions are surprisingly common. Globally, 1.7 percent of babies are born different to what is traditionally considered male or female, which is the rough equivalent of naturally occurring red hair.[1] If these conditions are so common, why do we hear so little about them? Why have the majority of us never encountered someone who is intersex, or know someone who had an intersex child? We believe the answer lies in the stigma associated with intersex conditions, a stigma we hope to help break by writing this book. The central factor in this issue is the rate at which children with intersex conditions have surgeries performed on them before they reach an age to give consent, before they ever know they were born with an intersex body. It is impossible to determine how many children born with intersex conditions are operated on, given the variety of traits that appear. Doctors are largely permitted to recommend and perform surgery using arbitrary sets of criteria. Gender is a highly complex and flexible identity, and yet doctors have been allowed to irreversibly assign gender to children, and surgically ascribe that gender onto their bodies, using subjective markers like the size of the penis or clitoris. For example, if your child was born with a penis that is less than 1.5 centimeters long, the doctors would likely recommend that it be removed and that your child be raised as a girl. If the penis is over 2 centimeters, then he would "likely" be raised as a boy.[2] Not every doctor would agree though, that 2 centimeters is long enough.

Putting it simply, whether or not the doctor recommends surgically altering your child's genitalia could depend merely on what one or two doctors subjectively think is an appropriate size for a clitoris or penis. According to one researcher, the medical management of intersex children relies "ultimately on cultural understandings of gender."[3] It is worth looking at the important difference between gender, sexuality, and anatomy, as historically the three of them were thought to be part of the same binary structures, but we now know it is far more complicated than that. The fact that so many bodies are born with wide variation suggests that our strict cultural conceptions of gender as it relates to anatomy are misguided.

The medical community is in part responsible for being very slow to respond to the idea that gender is fluid, and so are bodies. They rely even to this day on outdated, heterosexist concepts to justify surgery, as well as determine what surgery to perform. As intersex activist and author Georgiann Davis points out in her book *Contesting Intersex: The Dubious Diagnosis*, the American Academy of Pediatrics guidelines in the early 2000s instructed doctors to tell the parents of intersex children that their child's appearance could be corrected, and they could be raised as a boy or girl, as appropriate, and not to use gendered pronouns until a decision had been reached.

The factors that determined which gender assignment the child received was their "fertility potential" and their "capacity for normal sexual function," two concepts deeply embedded with outdated beliefs regarding gender roles.[4] Doctors, surgeons, nurses, social workers, and all other medical professionals responsible for administering care to patients have grown up in the same social and cultural milieu as the rest of us, and so it is no surprise that they subscribe to beliefs about gender and bodies that are problematic. We all have a responsibility to seek out new information and change our ideas when they are no longer supported, especially if those ideas are harmful. This book is aimed at all those who may have an impact on the care of intersex children, and especially directed to parents of newborn intersex children, who right now are facing tremendous pressure to consent to a surgery that is likely not urgent, or even necessary.

The largest barrier for parents of intersex kids, who wish to raise healthy, happy children, is the unnecessary medicalization of those conditions, the most dangerous of which is cosmetic genital surgeries performed on infants. It is impossible to determine how many children born with intersex conditions go under the knife, given the variety of traits that appear. Understanding the scope of this problem is not easy, as getting accurate data regarding infant genital surgery is problematic because there is no mandatory reporting of these surgeries, and researchers must contend with privacy laws and even parental shame when trying to seek out information. Likewise, the issue is very charged, so hospitals and doctors are reluctant to participate in research that demonstrates publicly the degree to which these surgeries occur. Nevertheless, there is data, and it supports the idea that, in almost all cases, a child born with an intersex condition will have a cosmetic surgery before they are one year old. A study published in 2016 reviewed all the literature on infant genital surgeries between 2005 and 2012, and determined that the average age for surgery was 11.2 months.[5] In 2016, doctors examined a group of 37 pediatric patients with ambiguous genitalia and found that 35 of them had undergone cosmetic surgery.[6] A study the next year repeated those results, finding that 25 out of 26 patients with differences of sex development surveyed had undergone cosmetic surgery as infants.[7] It is still considered very rare to withhold consent for a cosmetic surgery on an intersex infant, and parents who have done so will tell you how hostile surgeons can become when openly challenged. Although endocrinologists and surgeons have claimed these surgeries are on the decline, the data contradicts them.[8] Doctors remain largely permitted to recommend and perform surgery using arbitrary sets of criteria, and as a result, these surgeries remain common, and encouraged.

As we sat down to write this book, a story from the United Kingdom made its way to our desktop, which found that some intersex children born at the Great Ormond Street Hospital in London were being surgically altered without being given access to a family psychologist, a practice that directly contradicts the policy the hospital has in place for treating intersex children.[9] The very next day, researchers at the University of Huddersfield in the UK published a report that found that the National Health Service has continued to carry out genital surgeries on intersex children, without their consent, for two decades, which the researchers argue contradicts NHS medical guidelines regarding informed consent.[10] In spite of very vocal opposition to these procedures, doctors enjoy considerable discretion in recommending surgery. Every time we hear that these surgeries are decreasing, a story emerges that proves otherwise.

Any attempt to understand the paradigm between gender, intersex people, and surgery requires that we look at the tragic story of David Reimer and Dr. John Money. Many people have heard some version of this story, about a set of twin boys born in Canada in 1966, one of whom had a botched circumcision that resulted in his penis being accidentally removed. On the advice of Dr. John Money of Johns Hopkins University, a world-renowned psychologist and sex researcher, the parents of David consented to have a vagina surgically fashioned for their child, and they agreed to raise him as a girl. This provided a convenient case study for Money, who was theorizing at that time that human gender identity was "elastic." His belief was that a person's identity as either male or female had nothing to do with their body, and everything to do with how they were socialized. Here he had two genetically identical children, both born with penises, but one of whom he could now have raised as female, allowing him to monitor the effectiveness of his theory. Unfortunately, the experiment was a complete failure. In 1997, a Canadian psychiatrist who had been seeing Reimer as a patient, coauthored an article with an American sexologist, in which they denounced the standard practice of operating on the genitals of intersex infants, arguing instead for professional counselling in adolescence to deal with any psychological problems associated with their intersex conditions, assuming any problems were present.[11] Proposing a social and psychological solution to an ostensibly social and personal problem seems logical, and yet the medical paradigm continues to be a surgical solution to a social problem. At age 14, once he found out his medical past, Reimer rejected his female identity and began living as a man. He suffered from depression his entire life, and committed suicide in 2004. But by then the "success" of Money's experiment had been widely publicized. This flawed research formed the bedrock of medical justifications for surgery on intersex children for decades, and although Money's theories have been officially discredited, his insistence that children will be psychologically traumatized if they are left to grow with bodies that do not have traditional male/female markers persists. As we will discuss later, this problematic idea is widely used to convince parents to consent to these surgeries, even by medical professionals who know very well that it is a theory without any medical evidence or, worse, evidence to the contrary.

Cases like David Reimer's have left a stain on the medical profession in their dealings with people whose gender and anatomy are ambiguous. As a result, many human rights organizations, governing bodies, and medical associations have started to openly question, or outright oppose, the practice of infant genital surgery on intersex patients. In 2013, the United Nations special rapporteur on torture classified non-consensual genital normalizing surgeries as potentially constituting torture, and called upon states to outlaw "intrusive and irreversible treatments, including forced gender-normalizing surgery...when enforced or administered without the free and informed consent of the person concerned."[12] The World Health Organization stated in a report in 2014 that "full, free and informed consent should be ensured in connection with medical and surgical treatments for intersex persons, and, if possible, irreversible invasive medical interventions should be postponed until a child is sufficiently mature to make an informed decision, so that they can participate in decision-making, and give full, free and informed consent[13]." There are many more organizations who have come out recently against these surgeries, including the Gay and Lesbian Medical Association, The American College of Obstetricians and Gynecologists, the US State Department, and three former US Surgeons General, the latter arguing that, "research does not support the practice of cosmetic infant genitoplasty."[14] The American Medical Association board of trustees issued a report in 2016 arguing that cases of life-threatening complications associated with intersex conditions were very rare and, those notwithstanding, "genital modification should be postponed until the patient can meaningfully participate in decision making."[15] A resolution concerning that policy is working its way through the governing structure of that organization at the time of the writing of this book. While public criticism of cosmetic infant genital surgery grows, the number of surgeries being performed remains constant.

The most stalwart defenders of these surgeries are, not surprisingly, urologists, who largely continue to resist calls to end the practice. We should note that many urologists have come out against these surgeries, and we want to thank them for their courage, but we are still far short of the amount of support needed to end this practice. A problem for intersex activists is the fact that within the publications of urological medical journals, these surgeons have made it perfectly clear that the surgeries are controversial, and that their justifications are not supported, but parents of intersex children who consent to surgery repeatedly remark that surgeons presented the case for an operation without any mention of uncertainty or risk. For example, parents we have spoken with who consented to surgery on their children tell us how the doctors informed them that they would be able to preserve all necessary nerve function in the clitoris, yet those same surgeons published counter-facts in their own medical journals. An article published in 2012 in the *Journal of Pediatric Urology* concluded that "surgery carries the risk of disruption of the nerve supply of the clitoris."[16] This fact might come as news to parents of intersex girls whose bodies are still healing from such surgery.

Doctors continue to offer reasons for recommending surgery, and we will address those reasons in subsequent chapters, but at the heart of the issue is the belief that when a child's genitalia are different from what is considered socially normal or expected, the only solution to that problem is to surgically alter the genitalia so that they appear normal. In 2000, the American Academy of Pediatrics labeled the birth of a child with ambiguous genitalia a "social emergency," and urged early corrective surgery, while openly acknowledging that there was a lack of evidence that supported their recommendation.[17] Not all, but many of these doctors will claim that this surgical intervention is to make sure that the child has a healthy self-image, and that parents can give that child the love they need. The major problem is that there simply are no studies that support the idea that a child's mental health is negatively impacted by having an intersex body. In fact, as we will see, much of the research from scholars of gender and identity suggests that significant psychological damage results from taking away a child's right to consent to these procedures. Moreover, suggesting that parents cannot adequately love a child whose body is different from what they imagined it would be is absurd. Parents all over the world provide unconditional love to children with a variety of special needs, many of whom are not even their biological progeny, so we find it hard to believe this ridiculous assertion. Genital assignment surgeries on intersex children are premised on the belief that there is something wrong with these babies, which needs to be fixed in order for these children to have healthy psychological identities. But the real anxiety resides in the parents, whose fears about having a healthy child are often activated by doctors who then get them to consent to a surgery that they believe will protect their child from trauma, ridicule, depression, and anxiety. We understand that this concern on behalf of parents is real, and can be scary. We live in a society that does not understand variations in gender and sexuality, where doctors are beyond question, and where we fear what we do not understand. We hope this book can help unravel this complex of misinformation. Parental anxiety cannot override a child's fundamental right to bodily autonomy though, or justify overlooking the real negative impact that surgery can have. What is the psychological impact of being misled by one's parents, or by having doctors prodding and poking in the underwear of adolescents for no reason? When these children grow into adults and find out that they cannot have children, cannot achieve orgasm, can only painfully experience sexual intercourse, or will require multiple surgeries to correct the mistakes of past surgeries, what is the effect on their mental health? Should not these points be just as important, or more important, than the ones that suggest, without evidence, that a child with a two-inch clitoris will grow up feeling like a monster? There are in existence multiple organizations devoted entirely to connecting intersex people with one another in the hopes that, collectively, they can work to overcome the trauma of these unnecessary surgical interventions.[18] The negative outcomes associated with these surgeries, of which there are mountains of evidence, should not be as easily dismissed as they have been for years.

We, the Lohmans, are not only raising an intersex child, but also have professions that make us uniquely qualified to address many of the issues and misinformation that circulates on the issue of intersex surgeries. Stephani is a registered nurse, with degrees in Chemistry/Biology, and Nursing. She has worked as a clinical nurse, and has worked in a cell biology lab. Her knowledge of health and science research is extensive. I, Eric, have a PhD in Media Studies, with a focus on gender. I teach courses at the University of Wisconsin-Milwaukee, on topics which include gender in the media. We collaborated on this project, often discussing our memory of events or doing research together, but for the sake of continuity in voice and style, most of the writing was done by me, Eric. Our hope is that we can combine our expertise in this book to provide readers with a cohesive argument for avoiding any medically unnecessary surgeries on intersex children until they are old enough to provide informed consent, while also serving as a practical guide for parents or caregivers of intersex children.

What follows is part memoir, and part analysis. As a whole, this project will address many of the misconceptions about intersex surgery, both medical and cultural, that contribute to the perpetuation of these surgeries. We also take time to offer some strategies and insights for parents of intersex children who have concerns about how to raise a child this way. We begin by retelling our personal story of Rosie's birth, which includes our struggle with the medical community, and a discussion of how we came to the decision to wait on surgery. The first chapter gives some background on our family, and centers on Stephani's pregnancy and delivery of Rosie. The second chapter focuses on the aftermath of Rosie's diagnosis, and our subsequent interactions with medical professionals who pressured us to consent to surgery. The third chapter is an analysis of the common arguments given by doctors to encourage parents to consent, as well as their justifications for continuing the practice of infant genital surgery. We interrogate these arguments, and present evidence that ultimately refutes their rationale. In the fourth chapter, we provide what we believe to be the best argument for refusing surgery on an intersex child: our perfect Rosie. We share the strategies we have developed for raising a healthy, happy, surgery-free intersex child. The final chapter is a short conclusion in which we sum up our position and offer some recommendations for those in leadership roles on how they can help end these surgeries. Our hope is that our story of Rosie will help others see that there is no danger to the psychological well-being of your child to raise them in the bodies they were born with, and that love, understanding, compassion, and patience will do for your child what surgery cannot.

CHAPTER 1

Our Growing Family

It would be an understatement to say that Stephani loves babies. She loves other people's babies, she loves pictures of babies on TV. She's the person who everyone blames (and rightfully so) when a new baby at a family get-together is being hogged, or is returned to the parents covered in lip balm. When we met, Stephani had two children from a previous relationship: a boy named Deven and a girl named Delilah. We met in 2002, while I was tutoring children at a local elementary school in Milwaukee, the same school that Deven and Delilah were attending. Deven was in second grade at the time, and Delilah was in kindergarten. Stephani was active in the parent-teacher organization, and was frequently present for school events and programs. At these events, we had more than a few opportunities over the course of the school year to talk, but because I was concerned about maintaining professional boundaries, Stephani took the initiative in pursuing a date. Stephani taking the initiative is a reoccurring theme in our relationship.

We began dating regularly in late 2003, and progressively grew more serious. By 2005, we had moved in together. It was important for us to try to introduce the concept of me being a stepfather slowly. Even though both of the children knew me from school, and spent considerable time with me in the educational setting, having a new person around as a parent is always tricky. Nonetheless, Deven and Delilah warmed to the idea in time. Our marriage proposal was also pretty unorthodox. I was a jogger at the time, which was giving me chronic knee pain. In 2007, I was among the many Americans to be without health insurance, as I was employed only part-time as an intern while finishing my university degree. This job offered no health benefits. Stephani was working full-time as a lab tech in a cell biology lab, and had terrific insurance. One day while driving, I complained of the pain in my knee when I pushed the brake pedal to stop the car. Stephani sighed, and proposed marriage so that I could finally see a doctor about the knee. At this point, we felt that we would eventually get married anyways, but were in no rush. When you are older and have children already, the pressure to get married is somewhat diminished. We had other priorities. But being able to extend healthcare coverage added a level of urgency to our situation.

"Right now, it's only knee pain," she said, "but what if something more serious crops up and you are not fully covered? What then?" This seemed like sound logic to me, so we started planning a wedding.

Since we were getting married primarily so that I could have health insurance, it seemed foolish to spend a lot of time and money planning a wedding that would take place a year or more away. Our preferred option was to elope. We started talking casually with friends and family about planning a trip to Las Vegas to get married. Stephani's father was not keen on this idea, and he probably was not the only one. He eventually convinced us to have a small affair, and he agreed to do a lot of the leg work in planning it. He booked the hall, got the food and beer, helped set up, and paid for most of it. We basically just showed up, danced, and thanked everyone for coming. If you can get away with having a wedding like this, I would highly recommend it.

Our plan for children was always to have one child together after we got married. We thought it would be nice for the older children to have a little brother or sister that represented our blended family. Deven and Delilah were old enough to help with childcare, but not so old that they would feel more like surrogate adults than siblings. I had just started a master's degree program at the University of Wisconsin, Milwaukee, and I was reluctant to settle on a timeline for adding a family member. We already had a couple of kids, anyway, and I figured it was best to wait until after that two-year degree was completed and I was earning an income. Here, too, Stephani took the initiative. Whenever we would spend time with family, Stephani would enlist the help of others to remind me that there "is no perfect time" to have kids, and that "there will always be reasons to wait." Post-wedding family get-togethers became inquisitions into when we would have children, what was taking so long, and so on. Stephani's preferred response was simply to point to me and let me try to explain to a room full of aunts, uncles, grandparents, and cousins why we should wait. This lasted only a few months (possibly days?) before we agreed that we had reached the right time.

In early 2009, a few weeks after returning home from a trip abroad, we found out that Stephani was pregnant. We were expecting our baby around Christmas of that year. I was in the middle of my master's program, and we had decided that, after it was completed, I was going to apply to doctoral programs. We were eager to move to another city, if even for a little while, just to experience a new place. We had both been born and raised in Milwaukee, and needed a way to make a change. Naturally, this was not an easy decision. As we prepared to bring a new baby into the world, our extended network of family and friends were going to have only a few short months with the little one before we would have to leave. But we were determined to make it work. We planned that when the baby was born, Stephani would take her six weeks of maternity leave, then she would return to work and I would take over the childcare duties, seeing that I had time flexibility as a student. This was probably our first experience with volleying questions regarding our unconventional gender roles. People we knew really struggled with the idea that I, as the father, would be primarily responsible for the day-to-day childcare of our newborn. Admittedly, I was nervous at the time because I had never been the sole caregiver of a baby, but I also assumed that many women found themselves responsible for childcare even though they had even less experience than me and, if they could manage, so could I. Friends, coworkers, and loved ones frequently remarked that I was the "babysitter," as though the responsibility for childcare was temporary for me, assuming our arrangement was out of necessity rather than choice. This continues to be a persistent problem, and is illustrative of the degree to which all kinds of gendered expectations can crop up in unexpected places.

The pregnancy as experienced by each of us could not have been more different. Stephani was mentally well-prepared for what it would be like, this being her third child. I recall her being relaxed through most of it, calm, and thoughtful. Of course there was discomfort and difficulty, and I did my best to help where I was needed. But emotionally, she was my complete opposite. I was unprepared in all the ways she was calm, although I tried to prepare for it in healthy ways. I read a lot, and I listened to Stephani's requests. Although it's not clear who offered me this advice, I consider it to be the most helpful: "Your job is to keep her as comfortable and stress-free as possible." I wish I could recall who gave me this advice, because I owe them my gratitude. This bit of coaching allowed me to redirect my anxiety towards constructive purposes, such as purchasing several gallons of draft root beer for Stephani's birthday that summer. Throughout the pregnancy, root beer persisted as her one and only craving. She consumed it at breakfast, before bed, and in bladder-bursting quantities throughout the day.

Picking a name for our baby proved surprisingly easy. We created a shared Google spreadsheet and filled it with boy names and girl names that we liked. We would add to it when we came across a new one we liked, and we granted each other unlimited veto power over unacceptable names. The list for girl names was very long and contentious. Neither of us was particularly thrilled with the other's favorites. The boy's list was fairly short by comparison, maybe ten names total, and there was a clear favorite: Silas. Even before the anatomy affirming ultrasound, we were telling people that a boy would be named Silas.

Naturally, everyone would then ask, "Well what if it's a girl?"

"Well, we'll get back to you on that," we would say.

The ultrasound confirmed that our baby was a boy, and that the expected due date for our son was December 22, 2009. But that date came and went, and Stephani was very uncomfortably pregnant. Family members at that year's Christmas party fully expected her to go into labor before Santa arrived. New Year's Eve also came and went, but still no Silas. Stephani had long taken to sleeping on the couch during these later weeks to avoid keeping me awake with tossing and turning. For that reason, I didn't suspect anything when early in the morning on January 4, 2010, Stephani went to sleep on the couch. She was aware that the course of labor had begun, but opted to spend the early stages of the process peacefully laboring in solitude from the comfort of her own couch, rather than in a monitored hospital bed (or, worse, a hospital waiting room). By about 6am, she had woken me and said that we had to go to the hospital. Stephani labored for about an hour in the hospital, and opted to get an epidural as soon as it was feasible to do so, at which point the caregivers asked me to leave for the duration of that procedure, to make sure everything was sterile, but probably because I looked a bit aggrieved and no one wanted to collect me from the floor. I went to the cafeteria to have a cup of coffee, call a few family members and friends, and then returned in about a half hour. During that waiting period, I also found the time to submit one of my doctoral school applications, which I had been waiting to put the final touches on. In retrospect, it was all I could do to get my mind off the delivery and manage the anxiety of what was happening. When I got back, Stephani's progress had accelerated rapidly, and Silas was delivered within the hour. He was healthy and happy, and our family lined up to see the new baby.

Oh, Canada!

In April of 2010, when Silas was four months old, we found out that I had been accepted to two doctoral programs: one at the University of Minnesota, and the other at the University of Western Ontario in Canada. Moving to a new country is exceedingly difficult to do, logistically speaking, especially if you have no business in the country to which you want to move. Being accepted into a school though is one of the few opportunities that allows a whole family to pick up and move, get jobs, and live legally for a certain period of time abroad. We knew this might be the only chance we would get to live in another country, so we seized it. We accepted the spot in the Canadian program and planned to move on July 1, 2010. Little did we know that July 1 is Canada Day, a national holiday that celebrates the unification of the three original Canadian colonies in 1867. Unlike Milwaukee, and most of the US, businesses and stores actually close on holidays, so the grocery stores, pizza places, and pretty much everything else, were deserted. The absence of human life made getting keys to our new house, and feeding our movers, much more challenging than we expected. Our first day in Canada and we had learned a valuable lesson: don't assume you know what is coming.

We adjusted to Canadian life pretty quickly. The neighborhood we moved to was an apartment and townhome complex owned by the university. It catered to international students, mostly graduate students, and was located right next to the campus. It had a park right outside our front door, and an elementary school that was connected to the property. Delilah didn't even have to cross a street to get to school. She could walk home for lunch, eat with her little brother Silas, and return to school for the afternoon. Occasionally, she even had enough time to watch some TV while she ate. The student population of the elementary school was comprised almost entirely of the children from the adjacent housing complex, which meant it was not only racially, ethnically, geographically, and religiously diverse, but also had parents that were committed to education, being graduate students, and were extremely engaged in their children's academic pursuits. It was an ideal public school scenario for parents, teachers, and students alike. Deven attended one year of middle school for 8th grade, before moving to the high school. His middle school was fed in large part by our local elementary school.

I pursued a PhD in Media Studies, with a focus on issues of gender and labor, and their representations in the mass media. My program required that I take courses on a variety of topics related to the production and criticism of media systems. One particularly interesting course was Women's and Feminist Studies, with Professor Christine Roulston. One of the topics covered in this class was intersex rights issues. This was the first time that I had been introduced to the concept, and I found myself stunned to learn how the lives of intersex people were damaged due to surgeries performed on them before they could consent. In the course, students learned about Caster Semenya, the South African Olympic runner banned from racing because her body makes more testosterone than "normal" women. Semenya has endured a variety of humiliating interventions due to her heightened testosterone. In the past, competitors had demanded that Semenya retreat to the bathroom with a witness, and reveal her genitalia to that witness so that her anatomy could be independently verified. This is nothing new, as it had long been the practice of the International Olympic Committee to require female athletes to parade in front of doctors naked so that they could make sure that no men were competing as women. Even in the 2008 Beijing Olympics, Chinese officials set up a chromosomal testing lab to verify the gender and sex of female athletes.[1] Students in this course also learned of the David Reimer case, the aforementioned tragic example of the medical establishment's fundamental misunderstanding of gender and sexuality. We also read some firsthand accounts from intersex adults who have been physically damaged by surgeries, and I was deeply impacted by these stories. This is where I learned that some intersex people were subjected to repeated surgeries, and as a result they had never been able to orgasm or urinate properly. The accounts of intersex people who had wished they had not been operated upon left a distinct impression on me.

As people often do, I thought of myself in that situation, and resolved during that class that if I ever had an intersex child, or if I knew anyone who did, I would do whatever I could to protect that child from surgery.

In the summer of 2011, I returned to Milwaukee with Silas for a visit. While I was there, I received a surprise phone call from Stephani back in London, Ontario. In keeping with her tendency to unilaterally initiate major life changes, she told me that she wanted another baby. I was walking into a bookstore when I received this call, and I initially thought that she was just joking. It didn't take long for me to gather that she was quite sincere, and that this process was to start immediately upon my return to Canada. The idea of more children was no doubt percolating around in her head for some time, but I suspect that our absence (mostly Silas's absence) from London had pushed her over the edge. Having already had one child had taken all the fear and anxiety out of child-raising, for me, so the idea of having two babies didn't seem as scary to me as before. My schedule was very flexible. Since the day Silas was born, I had been responsible for the majority of the childcare. I was home for large stretches of time, and was able to fit in work (reading, grading papers, preparing lectures) while taking care of Silas. The idea of having another child around then, when I was already accustomed to this arrangement and comfortable with childcare, was very exciting to me.

That is not to say that it was easy. While living abroad, we did not have the type of help we would have had in Milwaukee, with grandparents and friends eager to pitch in and babysit. Fortunately, we had the help of two surly but amazing teenagers, and relied heavily on Delilah and Deven to help us with childcare. The first two years we were in London, Ontario, Stephani was working evenings at a credit card call center. She was home during the day, which allowed me to attend classes, and when I returned home she would leave for work. I would cook dinner, bathe Silas, put him to bed, and spend the evenings working and relaxing with my older children. One or two nights a week, I'd have a class to teach, and Deven and Delilah would help take care of Silas. I know for sure that we could not have gotten through it without their help.

As a former scientist, Stephani was not finding herself stimulated mentally at the call center, but jobs in research are hard to come by, especially for a non-Canadian. Positions in university labs often went to people associated with the school (spouses of faculty or fellows, graduate students), or were reserved for Canadians. Stephani's interests have always been in the sciences, or health and biology, and it came to her attention that the University of Western Ontario had a compressed-time frame bachelor of nursing program that could be completed in nineteen months. This was a highly competitive program, with only 64 seats available, and reserved for people with health degrees and work experience in health sciences. Many of Stephani's family members are nurses, and she long considered the field as her true calling. Stephani applied and was accepted to the program, to begin in the fall of 2012.

Stephani's plan was to time the birth of this child with the start of the semester. Canada's maternity leave policy is incredibly generous. People receive one year of maternity leave and, to ensure their population takes the time, the Canadian government gives new parents a stipend that represents a percentage of their wages. This meant that she would collect some of her wages for several months while attending school, and would return to work for a year or so while finishing the nursing program. Knowing things would be extremely tight for nearly two years, we planned to save up some money to help get us through, and hoped that my teaching wages would supplement the family budget to hold us off until Stephani could finish school and begin working as a nurse. This plan also required a fairly narrow window for Stephani to get pregnant. If she had the baby too early, valuable days or weeks of maternity leave would be used up before the semester started; too late and she would miss out on classes. Most important, Stephani wanted to have some uninterrupted time with the new baby before school got underway. It was a tight fit that we somehow managed to get right when Stephani got pregnant, with an anticipated delivery date of late August.

Delivering Rosie

The process for picking a name for this baby was basically the same as it was for Silas, with two exceptions. First, we didn't discuss the names we liked with family or friends. Baby name discussion on social media got pretty hairy. With Silas, we started "Baby Name Fridays" and would put up a poll (remember when that was a Facebook thing?) for our friends and family to vote on. We never really intended to be accountable to the names, and we regularly put up ridiculous suggestions. One Friday, we thought we would be funny and put up two terrible choices, Paloma Lohman (say it out loud), and Zoltar Lohman (after the coin-operated fortune teller machine from the movie *Big*). This caused a deluge of desperate inbox messages. People contacted Stephani from far and wide to beg her not to call her new child Zoltar, fearing a lifetime of bullying and ridicule if we doomed our unborn child to this name. Basically, when people hear the names you are considering, they all have an opinion about that name. Everyone knows someone they disliked with that name, or they think it will cause taunts from the schoolyard bully, it reminds them of their old flame who they would rather not remember, it rhymes with something, it has too many consonants, and so on. If you are considering a unique name, like Silas, people assume you are setting up your child to be ridiculed for a lifetime by having a difficult name. People encouraged us to pick a different name than Silas, and we briefly wondered if we should move on to a different name on the list. It is easy for people to do this when the person who is to have the name isn't physically born yet, when they exist in the abstract. But, ultimately, we decided to stick with it, knowing that when the baby is actually born, people are less likely to start questioning your name choice. Once a name sticks, it becomes associated with that person. You get used to saying it, and connecting it with that person, and it doesn't seem weird anymore. We love the name Silas, and now that he is Silas, he cannot be anything else in our mind. He does ask us to call him Max Power from time to time, and I do kick myself for not naming him that, because that is an awesome moniker. All of that being said, we sought to avoid that conflict altogether the second time around, and would only placate our friends and family with teaser names, just to be safe.

The second difference with this name selection process is that we wanted the name to mean something to us, to reflect something about who we are as a family. Stephani was over 35 years old when she got pregnant with this baby, which made her a "high-risk, geriatric" pregnancy. Mostly this amounted to early medical monitoring. At her second-trimester ultrasound, we learned that Stephani was pregnant with a girl. She was quick to remind me that ultrasounds are often wrong, and we should keep a boy's name on the backburner just in case. Ultrasounds that confirm a girl are more often incorrect, as well, since a penis may be underdeveloped or obscured, and so not seeing a penis in an ultrasound doesn't necessarily mean it's not there. Likewise, seeing a penis in an ultrasound is pretty straightforward. The fact that the ultrasound showed a girl was fortunate because it seemed the only boy name we agreed on was Silas. Stephani and I are both proud feminists, and thought it might be nice to pay homage to the feminist movement with the girl's name. I suggested we name her after an obscure Italian feminist named Leopoldina Fortunati, but was vetoed with a head shake and an eyeroll. Rosie the Riveter was probably a more recognizable symbol of feminist strength, and we both absolutely adore the name Rosie. My grandmother is named Rosalia, and so it seemed all the pieces fit. We decided to name her Rosalie Violet, and call her Rosie for short.

The pregnancy was far less of a public affair than it was with Silas. With his pregnancy, because it had been ten years between Delilah and Silas, there were showers and lots of attention paid. People were eager to ask me questions, see how anxious I was, and so on. Since no family were living with us in Canada, there was less in the way of showers and parties. The pregnancy was physically more difficult for Stephani though. The grueling stress of work, childcare, school, and meticulous planning had taken a physical toll on us all, but especially Stephani. It didn't help matters that the final trimester of the pregnancy was spent in the summer months, in a house with no air conditioning. I can remember more than once seeing Stephani sleeping pregnant on the couch, with fans blowing on her from multiple directions, with legs, arms, and hair askew. The final week before Rosie's due date, Stephani was off work resting. On the morning of August 13, Stephani went to see her obstetrician-gynecologist OB-GYN for a checkup, and she asked her if she wanted to deliver the baby that day. It was two weeks before her due date, but her amniotic fluid was on the low side of normal, and the staff thought it might be best not to wait. Stephani did not hesitate, jumping at the chance to meet our new baby and end this pregnancy during a relentless heatwave. She came home and informed me that we were to return to the hospital that evening and they would induce labor. We decided to avoid telling any family or friends back home of the plan. Since they were so far away, they'd simply be waiting anxiously for updates, and it was impossible to know how long things would last. Selfishly, we also wanted to avoid having too many interruptions from family members seeking updates. Delilah was happy to watch Silas as we returned to the hospital for the delivery. Stephani was hoping for a quiet, private birthing experience, and I completely agreed.

We packed up our overnight things and set off for the hospital at about 10pm that night. I can remember feeling the familiar mixture of excitement and nervousness as we arrived. They admitted Stephani, and led us to a private room that had a single bed, a small fold-out couch, and a nurse's station. The lights were kept dim, and Stephani was hooked up to the machines that monitor everything from the baby's heartrate to the mother's blood pressure. The nurse made Stephani as comfortable as she could and, after she administered the oxytocin to induce labor, they chatted about Stephani's previous birthing experiences, nursing school, and life in London. There is some dispute about what happened next. I do not deny that the sound of the quiet chatter, mixed with the slow, steady drum of the baby's heartbeat coming from the monitors, had led me to drift off to sleep on the couch. I contend that it was a brief nap of no more than an hour, but the duration of my slumber is not known officially. I was woken up when Stephani's labor had progressed to the point where she was experiencing more extreme pain. She asked for an epidural and, after a lengthy delay, the anesthesiologist arrived to insert it. This time I was allowed to remain in the room, although I wish I had been removed, since I do not love the sight of needles, especially giant ones that go into someone's spine.

If you want to feel useless, I recommend standing next to a woman delivering a baby. Even the nurses and doctors, who certainly do an excellent job ensuring delivery of healthy babies, still spend a considerable amount of time in a typical delivery, standing around with their hands in their pockets while the mother does all the painfully difficult work. The way that Stephani was laying, in a fetal position, had her spine pinched, which was preventing the epidural medicine from effectively reaching and numbing her pelvis. A considerable amount of the medicine had been administered, but the effect was minimal. The doctor, who was clearly scared to tell Stephani to move on his own, pulled me aside and asked me to try and get her to turn onto her back. This failed. Stephani refused to move on my suggestion. I'm not sure I could have convinced her to move if a truck was coming through. Finally, a seasoned nurse arrived for her shift, replacing the nurse who had tended to Stephani most of the evening, and asked me why Stephani was not laying in such a way that allowed the epidural to work. I told her that she did not want to move because it hurt to move. I informed her that when I told her to move, I got yelled at and was not keen to do that again. The nurse rolled her eyes at me, and went to the bed.

"Honey, you have to roll onto your back if you want to feel better," the nurse said, rubbing Stephani's forehead.

"This feels fine. I don't want to move. I told everyone I don't want to move," Stephani replied, without opening her eyes.

"Mmm hmm, here we go," the nurse said.

The nurse gently grabbed the arm that Stephani was laying on, pulled it straight up causing Stephani to roll onto her back. Stephani did not resist at all, to my surprise, and the sudden rush of anesthesia to her pelvis provided visible relief to Stephani's pain within seconds. Soon after, she had her eyes open and was able to converse with us. Now that the edges of pain had been dulled slightly, the labor progressed. More medical staff cycled through, the attending physician stopped in to say hello, while medical students chatted with the residents. The lights had been turned on, and Stephani was being asked to push. She was given a very large mirror so that she could see Rosie's head peeking through the birth canal. I rubbed Stephani's forehead, replaced a moistened cold rag to it every couple of minutes, and whispered encouragement to her. Before the sun came up on August 14, 2012, Stephani delivered Rosalie Violet. The doctors lifted our new baby up so I could look up at her beautiful face, and I began to cry. I kissed Stephani's head and told her that I loved her and that she did so great. She laughed, smacked me on the arm and said, "See, I told you those ultrasounds can be wrong." Everyone in the room was shifting their gaze between each other, the baby, and the floor, but no one laughed at Stephani's joke. No one even cracked a smile.

CHAPTER 2

Congenital Adrenal Hyperplasia (CAH)

As the medical staff prepared Rosie's umbilical cord to be cut, I took the opportunity to look more closely at Rosie's body, and noticed that she had what looked like a penis, but there were no testicles. I knew from my studies that this was a textbook example of an intersex anatomy, or ambiguous genitalia. Stephani's birth plan was for the staff to place the baby on her chest right after I cut the cord, but they took Rosie across the room to a table afterwards, and they kept her away from us for a disturbing length of time. Two nurses were standing over her with a towel, and not doing anything else. My mind was racing as I tried to summon the strength to say aloud, to Stephani and to myself, that she had just delivered an intersex baby. That strength did not arrive for several minutes. Stephani grew agitated, and asked why they had not brought the baby back to her. Politely, and firmly, she requested that Rosie be brought to her so she could hold her, but the staff balked. Stephani told me to go stand by Rosie, and to see what was going on, but I remember that I could not see her body because of the towel, which was probably there to both hide her anatomy from me, and to keep her warm. After two or three minutes, I went back by Stephani and told her that I could not see anything, but Rosie appeared to be fine. At this point, Stephani insisted on having Rosie brought to her, and this time it was more of a command than a request. The nurses wrapped Rosie and obliged. I took pictures of Rosie and Steph, kissed them both, and smiled. I tried hard to push down my worry, I struggled to figure out a way to tell Stephani what I was thinking. A large part of me was hoping that a doctor would finally break the silence on the issue and tell us something so I would know how to begin a dialogue.

It was clear to me, and apparently to everyone but Stephani, that Rosie was intersex. Stephani had only briefly seen Rosie's body before they swept her away, and she had a hard time sitting up after all the epidural medicine that they gave to her. It seemed like hours that

Stephani was kept in the dark about what was going on, but it was probably less than ten minutes. I was overcome with anxiety at that point. While I am embarrassed by my naive thinking now, at the time I was very scared that they were going to take Rosie from the room and rush her to surgery right then. The fact that no one spoke about her body and that they kept her away from us for so long fed this worry. I had the impression that they were preparing for something, but they were not bothering to keep us up to speed with what that thing was. During the course of my studies on intersex surgeries, I never came across an explanation or description for what happens immediately following the delivery of an intersex child. All that I knew was that many people had had unwanted surgeries as children, and that many parents felt railroaded or misled into consenting to a quick surgery, but I knew very little about the actual logistics of that process. When did all these unwanted surgeries happen? How did well-meaning parents make any decisions in an environment like this? I was mentally preparing for the possibility of physically intervening if someone tried to remove Rosie from the room. That was very clear to me. I was truly prepared to fight for my baby, because I believed that it was possible that they would attempt to perform a surgery immediately. My second concern was that Stephani might agree to a surgery on Rosie;

that she would trust medical counsel without listening to me. Stephani and I have divergent opinions on some issues. As a humanities scholar, my views frequently clash with Stephani's, as a nurse and scientist. It worried me that she might not appreciate the seriousness of the issue. When the senior pediatric physician on-call showed up, the nurses took Rosie back to the small table she was on before, and the doctor examined her. As he pulled back the blanket covering Rosie, he peered at her body from a few different angles, nodded, and returned the blanket to her body. He approached us, and with a friendly smile, cleared his throat and began to speak.

"Sometimes children are born, and they're not quite a girl and not quite a boy," he said. "In some cases, the genitalia is just swollen and it will subside and go back to a regular size. Sometimes they need surgery for that. With girls, sometimes it can be a sign that she has a serious condition. At this point, we don't really know. We're going to have to monitor the baby to see if there's any signs of this condition. If she were to have it, the condition is treated by taking a daily medication, which she would have to take her whole life. It's easily administered as a pill, or a liquid. A pediatric urologist will likely want to examine her to make sure that there is proper urinary function. So, I know this is a lot to hear. Do you have any questions?"

After he finished explaining the situation, it dawned on me that the thing they were preparing for was not to take Rosie away and perform a surgery on her. More likely, the long, weirdly quiet delay was the staff preparing to deliver what they probably felt was some horrible news to parents. People tend to worry about the possibility of having a sick child, but here was a child whose anatomy may be less than clear, and thereby the parents' ability to easily assign a gender may be less cut-and-dried than usual. I imagined parents being understandably upset about the ambiguous genitalia, wondering what it could mean for the future of their child. Their heads flooded with thoughts about sleepovers, puberty, boyfriends, and swimsuits. How would they tell family? *Should* they tell family? Add this anxiety on top of the worry that the child may be positive for a rare genetic disease that we know very little about. I assumed that this had been the experience of the medical staff, limited as it may be, with parents of intersex kids, and they were trying to broach the topic with us as gently as they could to minimize the emotional toll. Our principal concern though, as it would be with most parents, was the possibility of her being positive for any life-threatening condition, and not with her anatomy. We told the doctor as much. From the hospital bed, Stephani told the doctor that she was not concerned about her child being intersex, and that we were not bothered by any cosmetic ambiguities in her body. Actually, Stephani said, "Okay, I don't care about her genitals. Just give me my baby." In my life, I cannot recall a time where I felt as relieved as when Stephani told the doctor what I was so desperate to hear.

The room calmed considerably at this point. Stephani and I both relaxed a little, and the staff did too, having observed the conversation between the pediatrician and us. They could see that we were not particularly upset at the prospect of having an intersex child, and the room resumed its more subdued celebratory nature. It was early morning now, and they were setting up to move Stephani from labor-and-delivery to the mom-and-baby ward of the hospital, where they would be able to get some sleep. We decided that I should go home to get some sleep, too. I wanted to be home by the time the other children woke up so that I could tell them about the delivery. I planned to make some phone calls to family back in Milwaukee, tell them that Stephani had delivered Rosie and that they were doing well. Until we knew more about her condition, we decided to keep this quiet. Our family was miles away, and we knew they would want to be here to help if they heard that Rosie was sick, and we did not want to worry anyone until we knew if there was reason to worry. I hoped to add a few photos to social media, let the grandparents and cousins squeal about the new baby, and then return to the hospital with the other kids so they could meet their little sister. As my head hit the pillow, I remember wishing Stephani and Rosie could be home with me, and I hoped beyond hope that they would not have to stay in the hospital long.

A turn for the worse

I called the next morning to see how Stephani and Rosie were doing, but got no answer on Stephani's cell phone. I sent a text message next, and waited for a reply. When it finally came, Stephani said that I should come to the hospital, gave me the room number, and told me not to bring the kids yet because Rosie was not with her. As I drove to the hospital, I tried to distract myself with thoughts besides Rosie's absence. When I walked into the room, Stephani had just emerged from a shower, and looked upset. Her right leg was badly swollen from the epidural, and she had limited mobility as a result. A lot had happened overnight, she told me, and none of it was encouraging.

The doctors had taken Rosie to the neonatal intensive care unit as a precaution because her physicians suspected that she had Congenital Adrenal Hyperplasia (CAH), and that warranted close monitoring. Hours after the delivery, Stephani was still unable to walk from the epidural medication, so they wheeled her bed by the neonatal intensive care unit (NICU) to see Rosie, who was sleeping in a tiny plastic incubator. This was especially difficult for Stephani, who remembered feeling a mixture of sadness and guilt. The desire to hold her was overwhelming, Stephani said, but so too was the feeling that she had somehow caused her to be sick by opting to deliver Rosie two weeks early, when she did not have to do so. Had she waited to deliver her, perhaps the delivery would not have been so fraught with problems. This, of course, had nothing to do with Rosie's illness, but it was still hard for Stephani to shake the feeling that this was her fault somehow.

Stephani had been able to sleep a little, when the NICU staff called her to see if she could come to the unit and try to feed Rosie. At this point, Stephani was able to sit upright in a wheelchair, which she used to move to the NICU. When she arrived, she found that a NICU doctor and a nurse had tried and failed twice to insert an IV into Rosie's head. They had shaved a small patch of her head to do so. The nurse in the NICU told us that she objected when the doctor suggested shaving Rosie's entire head, telling the new resident that shaving a baby's entire head was unnecessary given they only needed access to an inch or two of exposed skin. The nurse kindly placed the auburn lock into an envelope as a keepsake, and gave it to Stephani apologetically. The next best option to a head IV was to insert an IV line into the umbilical vein. Part of Rosie's condition is that in periods of sickness or physical stress, her blood sugar can dip to dangerous levels. That is exactly what happened to Rosie after she was born, because birth is exhausting for moms and babies alike. Rosie's blood sugar was critically low in the hours after she was delivered, and they needed to administer a lot of steroids and sugar into her tiny body. This rapid loss of blood sugar was consistent with the disease the doctors believed she likely had: CAH. It would still be another two days before this diagnosis was confirmed, since the newborn screening that checked for this condition had to be sent to Ottawa.

The room was lonely without Rosie. A hospital room in the mother-and-baby unit without a baby is a bit depressing.

"So where is Rosie now?" I asked. "Can I see her?"

"Well, we have to leave this room, I think. I'm not really sure what is going on. A female medical student came in to check on me, and check on my leg. She said that as the epidural wears off, the swelling will go down. Then she left, and this male resident comes in. He sat on the bed, and said, 'This isn't a hotel.' I was completely gob-smacked. I didn't know what to say. I don't really even remember what I said after that."

"What the hell is that supposed to mean?" I asked indignantly. "Where are we supposed to go?"

"I don't know," Stephani replied. "But after that guy left, a nurse came in and asked where I was going, because she saw me packing up. I told her what the resident said to me. She looked irritated, and told me the entire mom-and-baby unit isn't even near full, so there's no rush to leave. But we obviously can't stay here forever, so we have to leave at some point. I don't think Rosie will be coming back to this unit anyway. I just started packing up my stuff and was going to go wait in the lobby, but the nurse said I could go put it in the room Rosie is going to be moved to in the NICU. I'm not leaving here without Rosie, Eric."

I knew she meant that not so much for me, as I already trusted that she would stay where Rosie was no matter what, but it was meant more to reaffirm this point for the medical staff, if they happened to be listening at that moment. Stephani had just delivered an intersex child who may have been positive for a disease that is very dangerous. We were unsure at this point what this could mean for her future health and well-being. Stephani had not been allowed to hold her much and, when she did, it was brief and scary. Rosie was connected to tubes and monitors, and staff were always milling about, asking questions and checking readings and signs. Stephani was never able to really have any private personal time with her baby that night. Rosie had been poked and prodded overnight, and Stephani could tell that the doctors were growing more concerned with her condition by the minute. Information was slow in coming though, adding to the stress of the situation. And to top it all off, an insensitive resident had taken it upon himself to make us feel unwelcome, for no apparent reason whatsoever. We were angry and scared, but determined to stay close to Rosie.

Adrenal crisis

The doctors now believed it likely that Rosie was positive for CAH, but were unable to treat it in the way they normally might until the confirmation came back. Part of the problem is that this disease is so rare that many of the clinicians on the endocrinology team had never treated anyone with this disease before, and were learning about it as we were. Another problem is that there are two types of CAH: the standard type means that children cannot make cortisol, which is a necessary stress hormone. The other and arguably more severe type is called Salt-Wasting CAH (SW-CAH). SW-CAH means that children cannot make cortisol, but also are deficient in aldosterone, another steroid. Aldosterone is essential for sodium retention in the body, and so when people are deficient in sodium, it can influence a multitude of bodily functions, including energy levels, cognition, and blood pressure. This was the more important confirmation that we were waiting for, as the doctors had already started to treat Rosie with cortisol replacement, but salt-wasters needed a second medication, as well as salt supplements. However, her condition was not improving during the interim. She continued to lose weight drastically over the first 24 hours, and was having difficulty staying awake long enough to eat anything. They fed her expressed breast milk delivered through a nasogastric (NG) tube leading to her stomach. Rosie's energy was not sufficient to latch on to Stephani and breastfeed, and the drastic weight loss necessitated a way to get calories into her body without her having to expend any energy actually eating. A fold-out couch was made available for Stephani to stay in the NICU room with Rosie, and the unit had a kitchen and showers for us to use. It was a very different environment than the mom-and-baby unit, to say the least. We were welcomed here, and accommodation was provided to ensure we could stay close to Rosie all the time.

During these early hours with Rosie, we tried to balance our joy at being close to our new baby with the fear and anxiety associated with not knowing fully what was transpiring. I could not wholly enjoy these early moments with her because I can remember watching the door obsessively, waiting for someone to come in with some new information that would upend our brief comfort, and send us roiling again into uncertainty and fear. At the very least, any misconceptions I had about the speed with which a doctor would recommend surgery were dispelled. No one even mentioned surgery to us for quite some time. The staff there were amazing: friendly, courteous, and welcoming.

On Rosie's second day of life, the pediatric urologist visited Stephani in the NICU room she was sharing with Rosie, and told her that he wanted to take Rosie to interventional radiology to determine her urinary function. For this test, they would insert a catheter into Rosie, and fill her bladder with a dye that shows up on an x-ray. They needed to determine if she was expelling urine out of her urethra, or if it was being refluxed into her vaginal canal, which can sometimes happen to girls with CAH who have a shared exit for the urethra and vaginal canal. Urinary reflux in intersex girls is possible, although uncommon, and it could lead to urinary tract infections, which carry a serious risk of adrenal crisis for kids with CAH. Although necessary, this test was undeniably stressful for Rosie, who cried and cried upon returning to the NICU room. Stephani found her to be inconsolable, and she cried herself to exhaustion. Given her limited energy and unstable hormone levels, the energy expelled during and after the procedure soon plunged Rosie into her first adrenal crisis. The doctors did not provide Rosie with the added hydrocortisone to compensate for the stress she would endure during and after this test. It was our first introduction to the severity and precariousness of managing the stress of a CAH child.

These first few days were the most difficult. We kept trying to feed Rosie, but she would never stay alert enough to eat very much, and we desperately wanted her to gain weight. It was also very important to Stephani that Rosie breastfeed, but she simply did not have the strength to latch on, and we feared that she was going to become bottle dependent if her energy did not return soon. Speaking with family back home was tough because we found ourselves trying to alleviate their concerns about Rosie, but the pictures we posted to social media told a story all their own. All had feeding tubes visibly sticking out of her nose or IVs in her belly. Nurses were seen hovering to check vital signs, and the unmistakable taupe wall paint and floral privacy curtains were impossible to conceal. Pictures with her brothers and sister were on the same couch that Stephani slept on at night, with tubes, monitors, and blinking lights always just inside the frame, waiting to ruin our carefully staged photos. Blaring fluorescent lights shone brightly, blanketing us all in white. All the while, the start of Stephani's nursing program was inching closer and closer, and we were unsure if the doctors would release Rosie in time for Stephani to start. Rosie's condition would not improve until the newborn screening test that was sent to Ottawa confirmed the salt-wasting component five days later.

The meeting

The "Consensus statement on the management of intersex disorders," first published in 2006, argues that it is optimal for families of children born with intersex traits to be treated by an interdisciplinary team of specialists that can work together to address all of the complex issues related to the diagnosis.[1] These are typically called DSD clinics when they are permanent fixtures at a hospital, or DSD teams when they are assembled on a per case basis, such as ours. DSD stands for Differences of Sex Development, or Disorders of Sex Development, depending on who you ask. This terminology, while imperfect, is certainly better than previous medical terms such as hermaphrodite, but it is not without problems.[2] Assembling a DSD team is now the standard practice for treating intersex patients after birth. Their creation is supposed to encourage different specialists to work together, communicate, and decide on the best course of action together. This practice, although not explicitly acknowledged, is widely believed to be a direct response to the criticisms that medical staff have received from intersex activists over the years, who have placed blame on hospital hierarchies that privilege the recommendations of surgeons. Because these surgeons are at the top of the medical hierarchy, they have typically been allowed to operate without any oversight or influence from other medical staff, who may have different specialties. The hope was that, by creating these teams, you would have a built-in control mechanism to prevent surgeons from unilaterally deciding on surgery, or pressuring families to consent to surgery, because any recommendation would be subject to open debate. In fact, the statement says that the team should decide on a course of action that includes management of gender identity, psychology, surgery, and endocrinology, before any recommendations are made to the parents.[3] The statement also includes a detailed legal declaration on the importance of informed consent.[4] We did not know anything about these DSD teams when our first meeting with them was scheduled a few days after Rosie's birth.

I had been spending my time traveling between home, where I was taking care of Silas, and the hospital where I was sitting with Rosie. This allowed Stephani time to shower, eat, or drive home to get toiletries and clean clothes. Our older kids did a wonderful job filling in for us while we spent the early days at the hospital. Delilah especially volunteered a large amount of time attending to Silas, which she did without complaint. I think she recognized the stress of the situation and rose to the occasion like a champ. I would usually spend the morning with Silas, and then would shower and go to the hospital in the early afternoon with lunch for Stephani. I'd find out how they had slept, or if there was any news on Rosie's condition. I would usually leave after a few hours, around dinnertime, so that I could see the kids before bed, maybe eat with them, and then snuggle Silas, and put him to bed before returning to the hospital until the late evening, where I would stay until Stephani went to sleep. I'd return home to try and relax a bit, before going to sleep myself, and then doing the same thing the next day.

The third or fourth day after Rosie's birth, the DSD medical team in charge of Rosie's care scheduled a meeting. Stephani told me the time to be there, and I routinely arrived, just like the days before.

"What's this all about, do you know? Who is going to be in this thing?" I asked. I was nervous about what to expect and, since Stephani was spending more time in the hospital, talking with nurses, doctors, and residents, I hoped she would have some insight, but she was as clueless as I was.

"I have no idea. If they got confirmation about the salt-wasting, they would have told us already. Maybe they just want everybody on the same page," Stephani said. We waited with Rosie until Mary, the endocrinology nurse, came to get us from the room.

"Okay, we're ready for you," she said. "How are you guys holding up?" She was bearing a nervous smile.

"I miss my bed," Stephani said, breaking the tension.

We laughed, and I grabbed Stephani's hand as we followed Mary through the unit to a meeting room.

Mary opened the door and entered the room, and pointed to two open seats at a very large table that was completely full of people already seated and waiting for us to arrive. The walls contained people as well, some sitting and others standing. The number of people in the room astounded me. It felt intimidating, and overwhelming, like being led into a lion's den. We sat down together, and nervously smiled at the faces we recognized. I squeezed Stephani's hand and waited. Mary began by welcoming us to the meeting, and speaking on behalf of the assembled group, she expressed how excited everyone was to meet with us. All of the smiles around the table seemed forced. Everyone could see how scared we were, and at this point I suspect that many of them realized that entering a room like this only added to our stress.

"Why don't we go around the room, let everyone introduce themselves and tell you what they specialize in," Mary said. "After that, they can go around and try to give you a sense of the care that Rosie is going to need from them. We're all happy to answer any questions you might have. I imagine you have a lot of them." Mary was very warm to us, and sensed our unease about the situation.

Mary went on, "We all know this has been a very difficult couple of days for your family, and we want you to know we're all here to help."

There were easily 20 people in the room. To our left were the endocrinology doctors and nurses, followed by a social worker, pediatric psychologist, and a pediatric gynecologist. Several residents were next to them, and directly across from us was Dr. Maria Sottosanti, Rosie's pediatric endocrinologist, one of the few doctors to see and treat Rosie from the first days of her birth until we left Canada. There was then a geneticist, her resident, and the pediatric urologist and his resident. Directly to our right sat the NICU doctors and nurses, the people in charge of Rosie's day-to-day care while in the unit. Others stood around the walls and sat in chairs off to the side, and we assumed they were nurses and specialists working as part of the team for those at the table.

The endocrinology team went first, and began by explaining the rarity and complexity of CAH. Dr. Silver, the head of the pediatric endocrinology department at the children's hospital, began by explaining CAH in plain terms.

"Rosie was born with a gene abnormality that prevents her endocrine system from making cortisol, which is a basic stress hormone, a steroid. This steroid is vital for her health, so her body continues to try to make that hormone, because it recognizes that her body needs it, but she cannot produce it. Think about it like a chef at a restaurant, where the chef keeps trying to make a dish, but is missing a key ingredient. He keeps getting the order from the waiter to make the dish, he keeps trying to make it, but without that key ingredient, he always ends up making something else, some other dish. At the end of the day, the kitchen is going to be full of a dish that no one ordered. That is what Rosie's body has been doing. The steroid that she makes instead of cortisol though, is testosterone. But unlike a chef at a restaurant, who can just throw away the food they don't need, for Rosie this testosterone stays in her body. This is why she was born with ambiguous genitalia, because, while she was in the womb, her body was trying to make cortisol and couldn't. Without that key ingredient to make cortisol, you have testosterone instead. The excess testosterone started to virilize her body as though she were a boy. Now, going forward, she will have to take a cortisol supplement orally, and that will stop her body from trying to make any, which means she'll no longer be making all this extra testosterone either. In a sense, if we go back to the restaurant metaphor, what we're doing is ordering out the dish from a different restaurant, so the chef doesn't try to make it anymore."

I interjected, "But that will not do anything about her genitalia, right? This is how it is regardless of the level of testosterone in her body?"

"That's right," Dr. Silver replied. "Her genitalia will not be affected by the reduction in testosterone in her body."

"So what do we have to watch for?" Stephani asked, shifting the focus to how to manage this complex hormonal balancing act.

"This disease can be very serious. If everything is well controlled, her day-to-day life will be normal. However, in periods of stress or injury, where our bodies normally create extra cortisol, hers will not, and it is vital to her survival that she have it. This means that you will have to give her extra medication when she is under stress, or sick, or injured. The difficulty for us, and especially for you as her parents, who will be responsible for the day-to-day management of this condition, is to recognize when extra cortisol may be needed. In addition, if she is a salt-waster, this could get even more complicated as it could affect her diet and electrolyte balance. I don't want to alarm you, because most days she will be easily managed. But there are going to be times when she needs special care, and that's the case for everyone with this condition. In her lifetime, I would be surprised if she had fewer than ten hospital stays as a result of her illness."

It dawned on Stephani at this point that Rosie might have a true disability; her desire to do some of the things she may want to do, like be an athlete, could be in jeopardy. She began to cry quietly, and I put my arm around her. Dr. Silver began speaking again, after a brief pause.

"We're going to closely monitor her hormone levels with weekly blood tests for the first six weeks after you are discharged. You'll have to bring her into the pediatric medical day unit here at the hospital for that. Then if things are stable, we will be able to space that out to once every two weeks, then once a month, and then hopefully every six weeks. She will need to get regular bloodwork for her whole life to make sure that the cortisol supplement is effective, and if it's not, then we'll have to change the dosage. I think you understand, this is complex, and the factors that go into getting the balance right are…not always precise."

Stephani took a deep breath, and asked who would be in charge of managing her hormone levels.

"Across from you is Dr. Maria Sottosanti, she's a pediatrician who specializes in working with kids that have diabetes. For diabetic children, the treatment is remarkably similar to what you'll be doing. There is regular medication delivery. There is frequent monitoring of blood sugar and hormones through bloodwork. Doses change as the children grow, and so on. Dr. Sottosanti has a lot of experience with patients who require this type of attention, and she will work directly with our endocrinology team. You're in good hands with her."

Stephani and I smiled at Dr. Sottosanti, who was looking at us empathetically. Dr. Maria Sottosanti was born 32 years earlier right there in London, Ontario, a full three-and-a-half months premature. She weighed only 1 pound, 15 ounces at birth and doctors at the time gave her only a 25 percent chance of survival, which was considerably better than other Ontario hospitals at the time, which placed the survival rate at about 10 percent for babies born that early. Ventilators kept Maria alive, and she slowly gained weight and strength in the care of dedicated medical staff. She chose a career path that brought her back to the same community that saved her, opting to work in pediatrics in London area hospitals.

Dr. Silver looked around at his staff, and nodded to us, indicating he was through for now. I understood why he went first, as his prognosis was the most daunting.

I wondered if they had arranged for him to speak first before we entered the room. Upon entry, the room had the familiar feeling that the occupants had just wrapped up a discussion about us. He smiled, and turned to Mary then, signaling she could move to the next person. We did not have any questions for him, as we were already overwhelmed with the gravity of his prognosis and, at that point, we didn't know enough to utter a single question. The next person to speak was the social worker, who was part of the child and adolescent mental health program at the hospital. She quickly made it known that our primary concern should be to shield Rosie from attention for the intersex traits. This was most unexpected.

"Does Rosie have any brothers or sisters?" she asked.

"Yes," Stephani said. "She has a big sister, who is 13, a big brother who is 15, and another brother who is two."

"My advice would be to be careful about what you tell them about Rosie's body. This really goes for anyone that does not need to know she is intersex. You especially want to avoid having friends of these older kids knowing and potentially spreading that kind of information around. Kids can be very cruel, and this is not the type of information that you want to spread around on social media, for example."

"I'm confused. My older kids are going to have to provide care for Rosie, changing her diaper, and giving her baths. I'm not sure how this is something that can be kept private. Are you saying that we shouldn't tell them about her body?" Stephani was polite about her confusion, but it was clear to me that the advice of the social worker surprised and irritated her.

Primarily, it seemed incredibly impractical to try to conceal Rosie's body from the people living in her house, helping to care for her. Again, our other children contributed with many aspects of childcare, and were destined to see Rosie's naked body a hundred times a week. The secondary problem, which Stephani saw right away, was that this had the potential to balloon into a bigger matter. There was genuine worry that it could lead Rosie to develop a deep sense of shame about her body. If people were secretive about her anatomy, or shielded her in a way they did not with her brother, who was only two years older, this could quickly turn into a feeling of shame or embarrassment with her body. Stephani explained this to the social worker, who listened politely, and nodded along, but did not seem persuaded.

"Well, maybe it's okay to tell them, but it would be best to only tell them what they need to know. Or at least take time to remind them that Rosie's body is private. You know, ask them how would they feel if someone blabbed to their friends about a deformity they had?" Stephani and

I were very obviously uncomfortable with this advice, but were amicable in disagreeing with her.

"I agree that not everyone needs to know about Rosie's body," I said. "I believe our kids will understand that it's not something they should tell people. But clearly, to us, it makes no sense to keep it from them, or from the rest of our family."

Stephani added, "Right. I think that we can sit them down, tell them what they need to know so that when they see her body they don't have any questions, and let them know that they should not go around telling people this. We can also write an email to our family in Milwaukee and explain it all to them as well. We'll send that to my Mom, my sisters and brother, and Eric's parents."

This settled the matter, more or less. The social worker agreed that this was an acceptable outcome, but it was clear to us that she had concerns about anyone knowing about Rosie's intersex condition, and cautioned us against using the term "intersex" when emailing our family about Rosie. This was the first person that we encountered who suggested that Rosie's condition was something to be concealed. It is possible that her advice was based on the assumption that we would consent to surgery on Rosie. As a result, it made no sense to her to call Rosie "intersex" when in a few short months, her intersex body would be erased anyways. One of the key aspects of infant genital surgery is a strict policy of silence about the procedures. The primary justification for surgeries is that the child will be potentially traumatized growing up with ambiguous genitalia. An extension of this logic is that children would be similarly impacted psychologically by even the *knowledge* of having been born with atypical genitalia, which is why parents are often told never to discuss the surgery with their children or with anyone else, in order to ensure healthy psychosocial development. However, as Kishka-Kamari Ford points out in her research, this is a mythology that many doctors, healthcare providers, and surgeons are convinced is true, in spite of there being no evidence to support it.[5] That being said, if the social worker was operating under this assumption, it is likely her advice was consistent with the general consensus that talking about atypical genitals could cause emotional harm to the children, and this informed her advice to us.

The pediatric psychologist was the next to speak. Her perspective was that, at some point in the future, Rosie would benefit from speaking to a therapist, but of course there was nothing to be done at the moment. Body image issues are present in many, if not all, adolescents, and children with medical conditions may require extra attention in this regard, she said. I asked what types of programs exist for intersex children, and her answer was surprising.

"Well you'll want her to have access to a personal therapist when you feel she is ready. A good rule would be to find a therapist for her when she starts to have questions. There is an increasing number of programs and retreats that exist for intersex adolescents. Places they can go to meet with other kids like them, which helps reduce the feelings of loneliness or isolation that intersex children may experience. There's also many online support groups where kids can speak to other kids as they move through the more awkward stages. These types of programs can have a tremendously positive affect. Lots of online parent groups exist as well for you two."

This was welcome news. We were not sure what type of psychological impact being intersex could have on our child, although we assumed there would be some even if we succeeded in raising a healthy emotional child. She still has to exist in a world that may not always be kind to people with differences of any type. But it was uplifting to hear that there were programs where, if she ever struggled with the social impact of her condition, she could find comfort in a community that welcomed her.

The pediatric gynecologist echoed several of the points made by the psychologist, in that the type of treatment Rosie would need depended a lot on how her body grew over the next few years. The gynecologist had a practice at Sick Kids, a world-renowned hospital in Toronto, where she had experience working with intersex children. That hospital has a clinic devoted to joint endocrine/gynecological conditions, as well as a multidisciplinary intersex clinic. She assured us that Rosie's condition, while very rare, was familiar to many in her practice and that care would be well managed. Unlike the endocrinologist and the social worker, the psychologist and gynecologist helped to alleviate some of our worries. The endocrinology team expressed the fact that this condition was quite rare and that managing it would be challenging as a result. The psychologist and gynecologist had a different focus and perspective, viewing the management of Rosie's condition as considerably more straightforward.

The geneticist spoke next, and was noticeably intrigued by the opportunity to explore this rare congenital disease. She asked us questions about our own medical history, specifically the presence of any other rare conditions in our family. She explained that Stephani and I are both carriers for CAH, which means we each gave Rosie one "bad" CAH gene. Luckily, when we conceived Silas, he received at least one good non-CAH gene from either Stephani or me, and so was not positive for the disease. Nevertheless, our other children are all potentially carriers of CAH as well, as would be other members of our extended family. The geneticist felt it was important, but not incredibly urgent, to notify those other family members who are in the age range for childbearing, and encourage them to consider getting tested for CAH. If any of them are positive carriers, they should have their partners screened so that they know if their future children may be at risk. At some point in the future, she informed us, she would like to meet with us and do some genetic testing so that we could understand more about our family gene history. We agreed that it would be interesting to have a more complete genetic picture of our family, and the doctor was clear that we could wait until things had settled down before pursuing this.

Finally, it was time for the pediatric urologist Dr. Gill Dukat to speak. He was a formidable presence in the room: tall and muscular, with dark features and an aloof grin. Up until this point in the conversation, we had never overtly stated to anyone in the group that we intended to forgo surgery on Rosie's body until such time as she could provide informed consent. Dr. Dukat had already informed us after the test a day earlier that there was no urinary reflux in Rosie, and that her urethra and vaginal canal were fused very close to the surface of her skin, which meant to us that there was no medically necessary reason to consider surgical interventions at this juncture. However, much of the advice we received from the assembled experts was likely based on the idea that we did intend to have surgery, as most families do.

The gynecologist, social worker, and psychologist all provided advice that assumed the possibility of surgery in the future. Nonetheless, we figured we would let Dr. Dukat explain the results of the previous day's test in greater detail to the room, and provide us with all of our options, both surgical and non-surgical.

Dr. Dukat began, "As you know, we did a contrast x-ray on Rosie which shows that her urethra is fused with her vaginal canal very close to the surface of her body, and that means she does not have urinary reflux. This is good news, as reflux can lead to many problems, including urinary tract infections and so on."

"This is very good news, it's definitely what we were hoping to hear," Stephani said. I nodded in agreement.

"This is very good news. And with that news, I think you have two options for where we go from here. The first option is to perform a single surgery that creates a vaginal opening and separates the urethra from the vaginal canal. And at the same time while she's under the anesthesia, we can perform a second operation to reduce the size of the clitoris to a normal size. I would recommend this surgery as the best option. It would be best to perform this operation when Rosie is about six months. The second option is to perform the surgery to create a vaginal opening and separate the urethra, but leave the clitoris intact. This procedure could also be performed at six months."

Dr. Dukat folded his hands and looked at us, quietly waiting for our thoughts. I felt my face grow red and hot.

"I'm curious why you have not suggested 'no surgery' as an option," I said, barely controlling my anger. I felt immediate bitterness at not being provided with this possibility. I fully expected, naively I realize now, that the urologist would say that because there was no critical, medically-necessary reason to have surgery, that we were one of the lucky parents. Unlike other families whose intersex children perhaps had severe urinary reflux and required immediate surgery, we had the perfectly reasonable option of waiting. There was no urgency by his own admission, there was no problem with urination, and this was the best-case scenario under the circumstances. Not only did I anticipate that he would provide us with this option, I expected a full endorsement of this course of action, as it was clearly the safest choice. I was mistaken.

"Because I would not recommend that option," he said flatly. His casual dismissal of our objection caused me to turn outwardly hostile very quickly. Stephani, who was already very upset with the entire meeting, was quietly staring at her hands, which were in her lap. I looked around the room, and noticed that many of the doctors and nurses in the room were avoiding eye contact with us. No one stepped in to help us, or provide support when we needed it. I desperately wanted someone in the room to come to our aid and cite some research, or provide an anecdote that would make the urologist back down, but there seemed to be a level of professional courtesy at work here, where medical professionals from another field did not step on the toes and disagree with each other, especially publicly. And this was a surgeon, an expert in pediatric urology; it was obvious that he was not going to be challenged by anyone in the room. The pediatric gynecologist was the only person willing to make eye contact with us, and although she did not offer verbal support, I got the impression that she supported our decision. Dr. Sottosanti had her head down, but it appeared to Stephani and me that she was upset by this situation. It seemed that the design of the DSD team had a limitation, whereby if no one is willing to challenge the surgeon in the room, then the team is merely there to serve him or her with an audience.

"You see, that's not really the point," I replied, my voice getting louder. "Your job is to provide us with all of the options available to us, and then give your recommendation, which we can reject or agree to. It is not your job to give us only your preferences, and ignore options that don't interest you." Dr. Dukat sat quietly listening, with a look of indifference on his face.

"I'm sorry, but it is possible for her to urinate normally without surgery, correct?" Stephani asked.

"Yes, that's correct." Dr. Dukat replied.

"So then obviously there are more than two options. She could have no surgeries, and that too is an option," Stephani insisted. "An option I feel that you have not taken seriously."

"How is she going to menstruate?" Dr. Dukat asked, as though he had stumped us. As though he had been anticipating our objections, and believed that this rhetorical question would end the debate at once. Stephani, however, was quite prepared for this question.

"First, how do you know that she cannot menstruate normally? She can pee just fine. Her vaginal canal connects to her urethra, which means menstrual blood and a uterine lining has an outlet from her body, the same one her body uses to expel urine. It may not be ideal, but there doesn't seem to be a reason to rush to have surgery next month! Second, she is not going to start menstruating for probably 13 years from now, so I don't see why we would need to create a vaginal opening for menstruation at 6 months old. If there is a problem with menstruation down the road, we can address it then." Stephani was now as visibly indignant as I was. Dr. Dukat seemed unperturbed by our umbrage.

"In my professional opinion, I would not recommend waiting as an option. It is best to perform a surgery like this before the child can remember. They heal faster. It is less traumatic for them if they are not cognizant of the operation." Dr. Dukat began to roll out some of the arguments that plague medical discourses on intersex infant surgery. I am not exaggerating when I say that Stephani and I were both in shock that he would bring out these arguments, which from our cursory review of the literature on intersex surgeries, had no merit. We had not done extensive research at this point, but what we found was very convincing, so much so that we believed that the views Dr. Dukat had were outdated.

"Where is the evidence for this? Stephani and I have reviewed the research on this topic and none of the claims you just made have been sustained in the medical literature. We have access to the same medical journals and scientific research as you, and nowhere can we find proof of these claims. Now I feel like you are being disingenuous to us. Beyond that, if you are arguing that it is a good thing for children to never have any knowledge that they were born intersex, I would argue that you are robbing those children of their right to know about their own bodies. If you perform no surgeries on these kids, you allow them to develop an identity rooted in diversity and individuality and difference. Making every body look 'normal' even though they are functional is nothing to be proud of, and frankly does far more harm than good. You may be the doctor that knows how to create a vagina, but you don't know the first thing about gender." Once I had finished admonishing Dr. Dukat, Stephani and I sat waiting for a retort. We felt ready to counter anything he said. We knew that we were on our own in this room.

Finally, he responded. "I can see that you are upset. Why don't we schedule another meeting in a few days when you have had a chance to calm down."

The second meeting

Stephani and I went back to Rosie's room to discuss the meeting, and were both incredulous about what had happened. How is it possible that a doctor could still subscribe to such outdated ideas about gender and anatomy, especially with the prevalence of counter-narratives so readily available? Is it possible that he's never seen or read any of the first-person accounts from intersex adults describing the physical and emotional horrors they've lived through as a result of unwanted genital surgeries performed without their consent? We were also plagued with a feeling of resentment that no one in the room, who could all see how upset we were, bothered to step in to support us. Surely we were not the only ones incensed at not being given the option to avoid surgery, when it was such an obvious possibility. We left with many answers to our questions, but an entirely new set of questions were raised, and clearly the issue was not yet settled. Dr. Dukat intended for us to continue this discussion within a few days. The respectful, professional course of action for Dr. Dukat in that first meeting would have been to apologize for failing to recommend we wait, and then to make himself available for any future questions we may have about Rosie. But obviously, he was not ready to give up on the idea of surgery, which both startled and enraged us.

I think it was immediately clear to us that Dr. Dukat was less concerned with ending the meeting to spare our fragile emotional state, and much more concerned with taking a recess that would allow him more time to better prepare to make his case for surgery. And even though we had made up our minds about it, we wanted to make absolutely sure of two things going into the next meeting: we needed to be sure that we were making the right decision, and we wanted to ensure that we would not be blindsided by Dr. Dukat's belligerent and insistent approach again.

Before the next meeting, which was scheduled for two or three days later, we sought out as much information as we could find, and we approached the information gathering from two different perspectives. As I am a more humanistic thinker, and Stephani is more scientific, we each set about collecting data from these two perspectives. I focused more on the legal, gender, and theoretical resources, and Stephani focused on medical and scientific sources. I was immediately drawn to online sources like interACT (formally Advocates for Informed Choice), and the AIS-DSD Support Group, both of which are organizations largely comprised of intersex adults who have suffered at the hands of a medical community that has failed to respect their autonomy. These groups were full of first-person accounts of the negative physical and emotional impacts of infant genital surgery, so much so that it was overwhelming and emotionally exhausting. For me, the possibility of Rosie enduring a similar fate was too large and unnecessary a risk, especially when the risks of doing nothing were all based on hypotheticals and conjecture. Stephani's research turned up lots of questionable content, but nothing conclusive. (In the next chapter, we detail all of the research.) In all, she found the medical research to be lacking in any justification for supporting these surgeries, and she felt a deep sadness for the parents that doctors persuaded to consent to surgery based upon this flimsy research. With our homework done, we felt we could attend the meeting with the medical staff and confront

Dr Dukat if it became necessary. If it was not necessary, then at least we felt comfortable with our decision.

The second meeting was to take place in the same room as before but, when we arrived, we noticed first that there were fewer people this time. The social worker, psychologist, gynecologist, and geneticist were not present for this meeting, and neither were their respective teams, seeing as though there was no pressing need for their attendance. All in all, the number of people was about half what it was the first time. Present were the endocrinology personnel, Dr. Sottosanti, the NICU team, and Dr. Dukat, who had a laptop open in front of him when we entered. Dr. Silver had big news: the results from Ottawa had come back and Rosie was positive for Salt-Wasting CAH. This was not *good* news per se, but it meant that they could start to administer the steroid fludrocortisone, which they believed would help with Rosie's lethargy, sodium depletion, and weight loss. The team was optimistic that with this confirmation Rosie would soon stabilize. This was welcome news, and we were excited to return to Rosie's room and see if there was a noticeable improvement in her behavior. As soon as Dr. Silver gave us this information, I immediately began to cry. The feeling in the room at that point was celebratory. Everyone was smiling, and feeling joyful about the prospect of Rosie's improvement.

Dr. Dukat was the only other medical provider in the room who had an update to make, and so he waited patiently to begin until after we had peppered Dr. Silver with questions about the complete medication regime we would need to abide by for Rosie. Dr. Dukat turned the laptop computer so that Stephani and I could see the screen. We found ourselves face to face with the image of a child's surgically constructed genitalia, which Dr. Dukat had operated upon only a few weeks earlier, he told us. The child was no more than 8 months old, and someone took the picture immediately after Dr. Dukat completed the surgery, while the child still lay asleep on the operating table. He clicked through a few more images, but I had since turned away from the computer. I looked at Stephani, who was looking across the table at the wall. I have no idea how many images she saw before she turned away, but it was fewer than I saw.

I have never understood what this exercise was supposed to accomplish. If he was under the impression that we were against the surgery because we believed he was incapable of achieving a cosmetically appropriate result, then I could see why he would believe that showing us his surgical abilities might persuade us. Perhaps he believed that we merely needed to see how "normal" he could make Rosie look, how "normal" she could be and, once we saw that, we would agree to a surgery. This of course was never our concern. The look of Rosie's body, whether it conformed to a cosmetic standard, or did not fit that standard, continues to be of no importance to us, so long as she is not experiencing any physical or emotional distress. Dr. Dukat did add a new layer of insult to the situation though, since it became clear that he did not attempt to hear or understand our objections at the last meeting, which I felt we made abundantly clear. If he had listened, if he had tried to understand, he would have never thought that showing us images of a perfect stranger's surgically altered labia and vagina would help win us over. In fact, it had quite the opposite effect. I imagined my Rosie having to endure the pain and discomfort I knew this child had experienced. I imagined a group of doctors photographing her body, and showing the images to reluctant, unrelated parents as evidence of the proficiency of the surgeon. I wondered, given her inability to cope with stress or injury due to the CAH, if she would even survive such a procedure, and why her survival seemed secondary to how her genitalia looked. I came into this meeting having considered these issues fully, but viewing the images increased our resolution, and further distanced us from a respectful relationship with the urologist.

While paging through the images, Dr. Dukat was explaining in detail what the surgery would be able to accomplish, but Stephani and I were both attempting to demonstrate, non-verbally, just how uncomfortable we were with this attempt. He noticed that neither of us was looking at the images, turned the laptop back towards himself, and asked us if we had given any more thought to his recommended plan.

"I must say, I'm confused about why we're being shown this. We made it clear that we did not intend to consent to surgery, and all that the extra time has done is convince us that you shouldn't be allowed to perform these surgeries on any kids, let alone ours," I said.

He merely nodded, and went back to his computer, signaling that he did not think it worthwhile to engage with me at this point. It was clear that he believed that this was the best way to convince us to consent to the surgery. We were both bothered by the fact that Rosie's doctor was so insistent on us choosing an option that was medically unnecessary. If there were a pressing medical issue, then I would expect him to give us an explanation of the problem and the proposed solution, but this was a cosmetic issue that we saw no reason to bother ourselves with since it was ultimately not our decision to make. This made the pressure seem all the more odd and upsetting. There is a simple question that Dr. Dukat, and many pro-surgery advocates overlook: what if these intersex children grow to like their body as it is? What if they like the way it looks and functions? This idea seems unthinkable and impossible to conventional medical wisdom, but it is an obvious possible outcome.

"I would like to see Rosie in about three months to reassess, see if there are any changes. We can do that in my outpatient clinic. I will have my staff send an appointment reminder to your home address."

"That's fine, thank you," Stephani said looking at my eyes, which signaled that I should not push back on him. In three months, Stephani would be in nursing school and I would likely be the person to take Rosie to her appointments. She did not see any reason to continue debating with Dr. Dukat right now, especially if we had to continue seeing him, and I could not argue with that. Dr. Dukat got up to leave without saying anything to the assembled group, and we let him. The NICU staff smiled at us, and suggested that we go administer the fludrocortisone to Rosie. By this point, most of the medical staff was aware of two things: we were very firm about our position on surgery, and about our contempt for Dr. Dukat. That day had the potential to be a turning point in Rosie's recovery, we had reason to be happy and excited at last. We were not about to let the experience with the urologist ruin that, and the rest of the staff were eager to join us in celebrating.

The NICU staff began administering fludrocortisone to Rosie immediately after we returned from the second meeting. It was no exaggeration to say that she was like a completely different child. She ate so much, it was as if she had never eaten before. She would feed from the bottle happily, which I loved because it meant I got to snuggle her, and look at her pretty eyes, which were now open frequently inspecting my face. Much to Stephani's relief, she latched on to breastfeed without too much trouble. The staff began discussing release dates with us, and I felt elated about the prospect of having my family back under a single roof. Before we could take her home, Stephani and I were required to prove that we could insert a tube in her nose that led to her stomach, called an NG tube. She still needed to have the tube for medication and feeding, at least for a few more days, but if we could show that we were capable of changing it, they would let us go earlier. Stephani was a natural, and inserted it with no problem. I, on the other hand, am more on the squeamish side. The NICU nurse showed me how to measure the tube, put some lubricant on it, and calmly said, "It's best if you can get it into her nose and passed the back of her throat quickly because if she starts crying, the back of her throat will close up and you'll have to wait to try again. It won't go down if she's crying."

"Got it," I said. "Just like a Band-Aid. Do it quickly. I got this." I did not actually. The first time I tried to insert it, I perhaps did it too fast and it coiled up in the back of her throat and came out of her mouth, which caused her to immediately start crying, ending my first attempt in utter failure. About thirty minutes later, after Stephani and the nurses stopped mocking me, I made another attempt, which ended in the same thing because this time, I went way too slowly. Hoping to avoid another crying fit, and wanting desperately to be successful so that Rosie could come home, I relaxed and got the tube inserted quickly and correctly the third time.

We brought Rosie home a day or two later, and were beyond thrilled to be back together. Summer was coming to an end, and school was about to start again. We found a solid routine, which had me home with the children most days because Stephani was busy in school. From the first few days of Rosie's life, she took her medication without any problems. We feel very fortunate about that. For the first year, Rosie had to take multiple doses of medication, and she did so without any struggle at all. She would get one milligram of liquid hydrocortisone solution three times a day, which she appeared to like. I would also have to crush up a pill of aldosterone replacement, and suspend it in water. She received this medication only once a day. Finally, she also needed to have salt supplements once a day, and this was about a teaspoonful of water that was five times saltier than human tears: a solution that

Stephani made herself. Rosie swallowed this horrible liquid without any fussing. She has been a trooper since the beginning.

CHAPTER 3

Resisting Surgery

Interest in the topic of intersex surgery remains high, but poorly understood overall. Certainly the general public is lacking in knowledge about it. Most people's first encounter with the topic of intersex births is when they or someone close to them actually delivers a child like Rosie, and they are facing a decision they did not even know existed for people. Perhaps this explains your situation, and it is why you are reading this book. Perhaps you are in the medical community, a nurse or social worker, a pediatrician or surgeon. If you are in this latter group, you may find yourself in a shifting environment with regard to intersex surgeries, and want to understand it better. In this section, we will present the reasons Stephani and I decided against surgery on Rosie by explaining and refuting the arguments typically used to convince parents to consent to intersex infant genital surgery. Stephani and I are both accomplished scholars, and it is our intention to provide a thoroughly researched analysis for why we chose the option we did, and for why you as a parent, relative, doctor, politician, or friend should consider doing the same. It is not our intention to demonize the medical community in any way. We have had many doctors, nurses, and staff that have been respectful and supportive of our decision. Even the doctors who continue to perform these surgeries are, we believe, acting with what they believe to be the best interest of the child in mind. We are human though, and we all make mistakes: *even doctors*. We hope to appeal to that humanity in us all to effect positive change.

Consider the arguments that follow, ponder the research, and initiate the changes where you can. If you are a parent of an intersex child, ask questions, push back, seek out other opinions. If you can delay surgery until the child can decide for themselves, then you should absolutely delay. If you are a politician, consider legislation that supports intersex rights, and limits cosmetic surgical procedures on children who cannot give informed consent. If you are a doctor or surgeon, demonstrate the courage and leadership that we depend upon; admit mistakes, take action to correct them, and remember your oath to "first, do no harm."

"It's best to perform the surgery when they are young"

In 2000, The American Academy of Pediatrics issued a statement that called the birth of an intersex child "a social emergency," urging early surgical intervention to correct any anomalies, while openly acknowledging in that statement that there was a lack of research proving positive outcomes for doing these surgeries.[1] There are two obvious problems with this rationale. The first is that doctors are suggesting a surgical solution to a problem that is social in nature, according to their own research. We do not recommend fixing social problems with surgery any more than we would recommend a social solution to a surgical issue. If your heart is not working properly, you need to see a cardiologist, not a psychologist. The argument that our urologist Dr. Dukat gave us is that surgery on the young means they will not remember it. The second problem with this position is that it is not clear to what the doctors are referring when they say that the children will not remember. It seems that they often conflate "not remembering the trauma of the surgery" with "not remembering the trauma of having been born with atypical genitalia." Both of these positions are simply untrue though, so it really does not matter which they are claiming. Surgery most definitely is traumatic in the sense that it can leave emotional and physical scars that may never heal completely. Clearly then, surgeries should only be performed without consent of the patient when they are necessary to preserve the life of that patient. If it is an elective or cosmetic surgery, which even urologists acknowledge these surgeries on intersex children to be, then the patient should be able to decide for themselves if any potential trauma is worth the outcome they seek. Suggesting that the surgery is traumatic, and so it is in the best interest of the patient for them to have no knowledge of it, is frankly unethical. Since when do we decide the right course of action based upon a person's inability to know or remember what others are doing to them? Instead, rather than concerning ourselves with what children cannot remember, we should be focusing on what they can remember, what they can understand and consent to. They should know the risks, know the trauma, and understand it fully so they can weigh the desired outcome against those risks. It is the job of the medical community to ensure that the patient understands these risks, outcomes, and side-effects, not to insist on performing the procedure before the children can understand these things.

In April 2017, the US Food and Drug Administration released new guidelines on the use of sedation drugs and anesthesia in young children. The report found that the exposure to general anesthesia and sedation drugs for long periods of time (three hours) or over multiple procedures could negatively affect brain development in children under three years old. The report concludes, "Consideration should be given to delaying potentially elective surgery in young children where medically appropriate."[2] The FDA's official position is to delay surgeries on children under three years old if that procedure is not medically necessary. I doubt that "not remembering the trauma of the surgery" constitutes a life-threatening situation that can justify such a risk. Make no mistake about it, this alone is reason enough to delay surgery on intersex children, given that their condition is very rarely of a life-threatening nature.

What surgeons are often reluctant to say aloud, but which underlies their argument for surgery, is that they believe they should perform the procedures early in order to spare the children the trauma of living with ambiguous genitalia. The child is different, they argue, and if you "fix" them before they ever have a chance to see that they are different, they will have no long-lasting ill effects. These ideas are laughably outdated, but persist nonetheless. Again, our urologist attempted to make this argument to convince us to consent to surgery in 2013, so rest assured these ideas continue to circulate. For example, one study from 1998 found that the policy of a pediatric team working at Sophia Children's Hospital in the Netherlands was to perform surgery immediately after birth, or as soon as it was feasible to correct virilization, in order to avoid "cross-gender identification."[3] In other words, they did not want the child to develop ambiguous ideas about gender roles, believing incorrectly that a person's gender identity follows directly from the presence of either a penis or a vagina. We must be cognizant of the situations in which medical recommendations are being made based upon flawed assumptions, especially assumptions about things that fall far outside the purview of the medical community at large.

Surgeons are not psychologists, and are no more equipped to give advice about the emotional impact of living with ambiguous genitalia than a psychologist is to perform heart surgery. As we now know quite conclusively, a person's gender identity—that is, whether they feel in their brain that they are either male or female—has nothing to do with their genitalia. The existence of transgender people proves this, as does a wide body of research in the field of gender studies. Therefore, the fact that surgeons often argue, even today, that you need to correct ambiguous genitalia before the child ever has a chance to be aware of their anatomical difference, or else they might develop unstable ideas about their own gender identity, is patently false.

Even the leading surgeons in the urological field acknowledge that intersex girls who have surgery before puberty will often suffer from vaginal stenosis, which is another way of saying that the vaginal canal will tighten to the point that the woman could not have penetrative sex without a second surgery. The need for a second surgery in girls with CAH was as high as 75 percent of cases, but is now around 36 percent. This statistic does not include women who suffer from stenosis, but can stretch the vaginal canal with dilation rather than surgery.[4] It is worth quoting pediatric urologists Lily Wang and Dix Poppas directly here, so that there is no confusion: "After early (prepubertal) vaginoplasty, many CAH patients develop vaginal stenosis and require vaginal dilation (only after puberty), revision vaginoplasty, and sometimes multiple reconstructive procedures."[5] In their own words, many of these children will need revision surgeries and actions to reassess the results of the initial procedure, which itself was not necessary, and which doctors performed before the child was a year old. Therefore, it is false to claim that it is safer to perform the surgery when they are young, especially if that surgery leads to more surgeries, procedures, and interventions. If the concern were "correction" before the patient ever realizes they have a different body, this is undermined by having the doctors perform multiple procedures throughout her life. If pediatric urologists are fully aware that multiple surgeries are necessary in most cases, then what is the impetus to have a surgery while the child is an infant, before they can consent? As few surgeries as possible should be the standard of care. Ideally, if a person can go their whole life without having any surgeries, that would be the safest for them from both a physical and emotional standpoint. Naturally, given the risk involved with anesthetizing children under three, and the fact that multiple surgeries and procedures are almost always needed once a child has a single surgery, there simply is no justification for performing these procedures in infancy.

One of the oft-overlooked aspects of this argument is that while a surgery may be able to "correct" ambiguous genitalia in children, it does nothing to address other related components to the conditions, which may also present embarrassing or unwanted issues. Girls with CAH, for example, can have irregular or nonexistent periods, may be prone to unwanted facial hair and, as a group, have higher rates of same-sex attraction than the general population.[6] If the doctor's principle concern is that children with ambiguous genitalia will not have a stable gender identity without surgery, then what is to be done to address the effects of, say, female facial hair, or an inability to have a period, which no doubt would have a similar influence on "cross-gender identification"? Children who have surgeries when they are infants may still experience these other aspects, and will likely have questions or concerns that create problems for the idea of stable gender identification. Our goal then should not be to try to stamp out difference in our children, but welcome it, accept it, and teach others to do the same. In fact, the American College of Obstetricians and Gynecologists, and the American Society for Pediatric and Adolescent Gynecology, both argue that when adolescents request surgery for cosmetically abnormal, but functional genitalia, doctors refer the patient first to a counsellor who can help them learn to accept their body as it is. Education, support, and reassurance from a therapist is the standard of care for teens with body image issues that result from atypical genitalia, and only after therapy, if problems persist, is surgery even considered. This group also reminds surgeons in the report that it is a violation of US law to alter the labia or clitoris of a child under 18 years old if the procedure is not medically necessary (a statute that continues to go unnoticed).[7]

The position that we hold is that even if a child were to grow up with feelings that were not strictly male or strictly female, that would not be such a terrible outcome.

Although there is no evidence to support the argument that children with untreated ambiguous genitalia develop a psychological identity that defies firm gender labeling, if it were true it is unreasonable to designate that as traumatic without any evidence. This sheds light on our prejudices about difference, assuming that anyone that does not perfectly embody the preferred norms and standards of our society is destined to lead a deeply unhappy, traumatic life. The burden rests on us as a society to accept variations within our population, not with the individual to change themselves to fit an arbitrary standard.

"We don't want them to be bullied"

We would be lying if we said that an intersex child is not going to face unwanted attention later in life because of their condition. As a parent, this fear is genuine, and we do not want to dismiss it. One argument we have heard from other parents of intersex children is that, while families may be accepting and loving of our children no matter their condition, the world at large is not always so kind. Parents fear sending their children out into a world they know to be occasionally cruel with a condition that marks them as potentially different. This is a tough outlook, but we believe there is another way to look at this situation.

An intersex activist in the 1990s was being interviewed about this situation, and remarked that just because our society is not always accepting of difference does not justify taking steps to change people at birth. "It's difficult to be Black in this culture, too, but we don't bleach the skin of Black babies," the activist said.[8] Living with any stigma or mark that society treats as inferior can be challenging, but we do not intervene in all of those cases in the way we do with intersex children. Imagine a child born with a hand that was completely functional, but cosmetically different in some way. Could you imagine doctors encouraging the parents to consent to a drastic surgery to correct the look of the hand while the baby is only three or four months old? The parents would likely believe that the child can decide later if he or she wants a cosmetic procedure to make the hand look "normal," but so long as the hand functions, there is no rush. In fact, even with slightly limited mobility in the hand, we doubt that the first option would be immediate surgical intervention. The recommendation of the surgeon might even be to simply wait and see, let the child adapt and learn to use the hand, and maybe they will become so proficient that they never bother with a surgery. At the end of the day, no one can predict what the individual will want later in life, so it is best practice to wait and let them decide when they are old enough. Certainly, the parents would consider that kids at school may make fun of the child, but they would take reasonable steps to mitigate the effects, opting instead to try and raise a child with the self-confidence to withstand such attention. Now consider if performing the surgery had the likelihood of actually diminishing the function of the hand. In this scenario, we imagine it would be near impossible to find a doctor willing to perform such a surgery on an infant. Or, what if the parents were told that having one surgery would likely lead to a need for more surgeries, physical therapy, and monitoring? In spite of similar concerns, surgery remains the most common treatment for intersex children.

If anyone believes that you can stop others from bullying your kids, that they can be protected from unkind people, or prejudices, or insecurity, simply by making them appear as "normal" and ordinary as possible, then you are mistaken. As much as we would like it, we cannot protect children from bullying any more than we can make other people friendlier, but you can soften the effects of bullying by supporting your child's self-esteem. Study after study has found that the best way to temper the effects of bullying on children is for parents (and teachers, or other caregivers) to remain highly involved in supporting those kids as they attempt to navigate their environment. Offering social support such as simply listening, providing advice, and helping children problem solve can greatly reduce the likelihood of depression in bullied children.[9]

The real psychological danger though lies not in intersex children being bullied by peers, it is the shame, humiliation, and mistrust they feel towards parents and doctors who mislead them about the nature of their conditions. Sharon E. Preves conducted a series of interviews with intersex people, and published the results in a book entitled *Intersex and Identity: The Contested Self* (2003). The accounts of intersex adults in the book paint a very convincing picture of the shame and humiliation that resulted from unnecessary medical interventions on their bodies as children. Conversations with doctors and parents continually revisit the idea that there was an abnormality that had to be fixed, which has a lasting impact on children as they grow into adulthood. Children internalize these feelings of inadequacy and abnormality when they hear parents and doctors discussing "corrections," which foster deeper feelings of shame as they age. Preves found in her research that intersex adults experienced three types of messaging that led to emotional trauma, which followed directly from unnecessary medical interventions. The three messages are, "1. that they were objects of study, 2. they were not to know the nature of their conditions or why they were receiving medical treatment, and 3. that such procedures were in their best interest and should remain uncontested and undisclosed."[10] One of the major problems with having these surgeries on children is that it is very difficult to appear supportive of your child unconditionally when they know that you did not leave their bodies as they were when they were born. It is equally difficult to make them feel supported when you do not fully express what their medical history is or honestly communicate what their condition entails, and when you prohibit them from consenting to the interventions that they have to endure. Preves' book is filled with first-person stories of doctors refusing to explain surgical procedures to adolescents, of kids having their genitals photographed and prodded while thirty or forty people stand around, staring. Interviewees retell how they felt lied to, or were told to simply trust what was happening because it was in their best interest. In short, there is clear evidence that intersex children are at risk of social trauma, but rather than the culprits being friends or classmates, it is doctors and parents who they feel inflicted the most emotional harm on them.

There is a bright side to this research, though. Preves found that intersex adults described feeling relief, acceptance, and pride in themselves when they were given a complete medical explanation of their condition, when they were able to openly share their body difference with others, and when they found other intersex people like them with whom they could share their experiences.[11] We cannot put our kids in a bubble and ensure they never feel the sting of unkind people, but we can prepare them for that eventuality by instilling in them the self-confidence and love to weather that storm and come out stronger. The surgeries have the opposite effect to what the original argument claims. Instead of "correcting" their body so that they feel normal, they lead many of them to have feelings of shame and inadequacy that they likely would not have if their bodies were left intact. If their parents sought to communicate self-love and bodily autonomy in their kids, they would do more to soften the impact of bullying than any surgery could. If we want intersex children to grow into healthy, emotionally secure adults, then refusing surgery because we love them the way they are will yield far better results. Give them open, honest answers about their body, encourage them to love themselves as they were made, and to talk freely about their body with whomever they want. One's body should be a source of joy and pride, not shame or secrecy. And always remind them that they have a say in who knows about their body, and what is done to it. Finally, ensure they know that there are many people just like them, and at an appropriate time, they can connect with them.

"It's just tissue"

In our experience, one of the most patently false arguments for why parents should consent to surgery on intersex girls is that the clitoris, which is often enlarged in girls with CAH, is nothing more than extra tissue. In conversations with parents of intersex children, we have found that this argument continues to crop up, despite there being sound medical evidence to the contrary. For example, a study from 2003 of women with CAH who had surgery as children found that their clitoral sensation was incredibly inconsistent compared with women who had no surgeries, and this inconsistent ability to feel sensations diminished their ability to achieve an orgasm.[12] The authors of that study acknowledge that raising a child with an enlarged clitoris may be challenging, "but on reaching adulthood the woman may resent the destruction of a major part of her sexual potential."[13] Leading surgeons in pediatric urology, who make their livings doing these surgeries, are speaking out of both sides of their mouths in this regard. On the one hand, they are telling parents that removing part of the clitoris is simply a matter of excising extra tissue, while in their own medical journals they contend that the clitoris is in fact highly sensitive erectile tissue full of complex nerves essential for sexual stimulation.

How is it that so many parents are under the mistaken impression that clitoral tissue can be easily cut without affecting sensation unless doctors were telling them this? One parent confided in Stephani that one of the leading urological surgeons performing the lion's share of genital cosmetic surgeries on infants with CAH told her that the enlarged clitoris was just like an "extra digit" and removing it was no more traumatic than removing an extra pinky toe. There has never been a study that provided evidence to support the claim that doctors can reduce the size of a clitoris and preserve sexual function and clitoral sensation.[14] This is what makes the claim that an enlarged clitoris can be surgically reduced without causing damage so vexing. Even a cursory look into the medical journals shows that the surgeons making these claims in front of parents do not believe it to be entirely true. Certainly, as medical procedures, technology, and techniques increase in quality, so too do outcomes for patients. But, as of right now, there is no way to have a surgery like this without diminishing sexual function and sensation, and there may never be a time when it is completely without risk. That is why it is so important that a person wishing to have a surgery like this must be given the chance to weigh the risks, and decide for themselves if it is worth it.

"Surgery prevents urinary tract infections"

Surgeons who use this justification are being either negligent or dishonest, as the medical literature has proven this to be conclusively untrue. A pair of the pediatric urologists who perform intersex infant surgeries, primarily on girls with CAH, published a review of the literature on intersex infant surgeries, and found that, "While all surgery is associated with potential postoperative infections, girls with CAH who have a common urogenital sinus are not predisposed to urinary tract infections (UTIs) prior to surgery. However, postsurgical complications such as vaginal stenosis may increase infectious complications in CAH girls as they get older."[15] The looming threat of UTIs is another popular justification utilized for these surgeries, which is strange given that the studies published by pediatric urologists have shown that UTIs are not a problem for the average intersex child until *after* they have had surgery to prevent infections. Another study found that in a group of 71 CAH children, nine had a history of UTIs. Of that nine, eight were girls, and seven of the eight had infant genital surgery. The conclusion of the study was straightforward: "our results do not suggest an increase in UTIs if surgery is delayed."[16] They are implying, of course, that there may be good reason to believe that surgeries actually *increase* the risk of UTIs, although the surgeons tiptoe around making that claim outright.

Typically, the *possibility* of UTI is used to justify surgery in girls with CAH, in the same way that the *possibility* of cancer is used as justification for removing the gonads of girls with Androgen Insensitivity Syndrome but, in both cases, the likelihood is less than 1 percent. Imagine that a doctor told you that there was a 1 percent chance that your infant could develop cancer in a vital organ later on in life, and the surgeon recommends immediate removal. It is absurd that any doctor would seriously make such a recommendation and be able to continue to practice medicine. Standards of healthcare assume no need for intrusion until a problem presents itself and intervention becomes medically necessary. Never have we arbitrarily removed organs and altered physiology based upon a mere possibility that a problem could occur at some point in the future, especially when that likelihood is the same across the entire population. Your body is just as likely to develop a UTI as a girl with CAH, so why do surgeons routinely subject them to surgery to "prevent" these infections, while leaving the rest of us alone? Patients can elect to have myriad procedures that are cosmetic in nature, or could be safely delayed; however, the patient's informed consent is required in these cases. In short, if a medical procedure is non-life threating, then the patient must be able to provide informed consent before the intervention. This is not happening with intersex children. As Chicago-based intersex activist and filmmaker Pidgeon Pagonis is fond of saying, "surgeons who treat intersex conditions should be treated like firefighters: if we have a problem, we'll let you know. Don't call us, we'll call you. Don't drive around looking for fires."[17]

"We have to remove these organs because they may become cancerous"

In the case of Complete Androgen Insensitivity Syndrome (CAIS), this argument appears often to justify the removal of undescended testes in the abdomen of women. Like the argument about UTIs in girls with CAH, the likelihood of these organs becoming cancerous is no different for CAIS patients than it is for the population at large. The chances of these undescended testes becoming cancerous is greater, and yet several CAIS patients we spoke with told us that the doctors made it sound as though cancer was a certainty if the organs were not removed.

Doctors rarely discuss the side-effects of removing these organs with parents or patients. Once they utter the word "cancer", many patients are so frightened that they will consent to almost anything. A study published in 2017 found that the risk of gonadal cancer in AIS patients is extremely low before they reach puberty, and even after puberty the risks are unknown (probably given the rate at which these gonads are removed). The researchers recommend that bi-annual screening is done in women with AIS in order to monitor the gonads for the development of any cancerous cells.[18] This course of action is more consistent with medical standards for treating everything else, especially cancer. For example, the American Cancer Society has recommendations and guidelines for cancer screenings that take into account risk factors, age, and available data. Women over 40 are at a higher risk for breast cancer, and the American Cancer Society recommends annual MRIs and mammograms, unless the woman has certain risk factors, which may change the recommendations to bi-annual screenings starting at an earlier age.[19] Likewise for cervical cancer screenings, prostate cancer, and various other types. The point is that medical researchers have weighed the actual risks of developing cancer, and used that to develop screening guidelines that seek to protect patients while avoiding or minimizing any unnecessary medical interventions. If a patient can live a normal life, while maintaining appropriate vigilance given their cancer risk factors, then that is the best outcome. We are simply asking that similar standards be applied to AIS patients. If undescended gonads in the abdomen of AIS women are at a higher risk of cancer, then they should be monitored regularly and removed if and only if they become cancerous. Removing these organs should not be a decision reached so casually, or without informed consent, given that doing so requires the patient to go on lifelong hormone replacement therapy and renders them sterile, having removed their sex organs.

"Parents want these surgeries"

Both doctors and parents of intersex children who have had surgery use this justification, but it is perhaps the most flimsy of them all. If we start from the perspective of the doctors, we would be remiss to find an analogous situation in which the desire of one person supersedes the rights of the patient to make a decision for themselves. The only exception is when a person is incapable of making a decision about their care, and the health of the patient is in immediate jeopardy. For example, doctors and loved ones can make decisions regarding a patient who has been in an accident and cannot give informed consent. In these cases, of course, the medical staff is permitted to do only what is necessary to save the patient's life. This is very different from the situation with pediatric surgeons who claim that parents have pressured *them* to perform these surgeries on their kids, insisting that the parents desperately want their children to look "normal."

We do not doubt that this is true, but we reject the idea that this is a solid justification for continuing the practice. It is perhaps the most cowardly explanation that surgeons have given. Since when do doctors perform medically unnecessary procedures, with full knowledge that the operation could have disastrous consequences, simply because a determined parent is advocating for it? Where do we draw the line? If parents can demand a surgeon cosmetically alter their children's genitalia during infancy in order to conform to adult heterosexual standards of beauty, then why not breast implants, eyelash implants, or lip injections? It is possible for children under 18 to get rhinoplasties or breast augmentation surgeries, but the American Society of Pediatric Surgeons (ASPS) recommends waiting until the child's breasts or nose are fully developed before conducting these surgeries. Their guidelines for cosmetic surgery on children suggests that the best outcomes are achieved when the child initiates the request for surgery on their own, that they have sufficient maturity to understand the risks and give informed consent, and that they have realistic goals. Furthermore, the ASPS has a detailed statement on informed consent for minors. The statement reads: "surgery should be discussed and understood by the patient as well as the patient's parents or guardian, including: details of the surgery, benefits, possible consequences and side-effects of the operation, potential risks and adverse outcomes as well as their probability and severity; alternatives to the procedure being considered and their benefits, risks and consequences; and the anticipated outcome."[20] Our own experience with the pediatric urologist pushing for surgery on Rosie was that he never bothered to discuss the consequences or risks of the operation at all. We had to raise them ourselves, and when we did, he downplayed or ignored them. The idea that Rosie should be emotionally mature enough to consent to any cosmetic procedure on her body escaped consideration by the surgeon completely.

The CARES Foundation, a leading CAH advocacy group, has repeatedly made the claim that they do not support a ban on intersex infant surgeries because they want to preserve the "rights" of parents to choose a surgical option for their children. There is a lot of talk of protecting the rights of the parents, but this is noticeably flawed. To state the obvious, it is not, nor has it ever been, the legal right of a parent to consent to a cosmetic medical procedure on a child who cannot provide informed consent. The US has a law against the practice of operating on female genitals of children under 18 when the procedure is not medically necessary. The United

Nations Committee on the Rights of Children called for a governmental prohibition on the "harmful medical practices on intersex children, including unnecessary surgery and treatment without their informed consent."[21] We already place many limitations on what parents are allowed to do to their children, what decisions they can make for them, especially when those decisions may have lasting consequences on the life of that individual. This is not the parent's right, it has never been the parent's right, and it should not be treated as such. That is the child's right, and only theirs. Our job as parents, as doctors, as policy makers, is to preserve that sacred right for the individual child.

"They have XX chromosomes: they're girls"

When it comes to girls with CAH, a major argument for surgery rests on essentialist claims about gender and anatomy. Given the fact that all of the typical physical markers of gender indicates that they are girls, they argue that the surgery is not about picking a gender for an intersex person, but making the genitalia conform to their existing gender. So the child may have a uterus, they have XX chromosomes, they will menstruate and can bear children, they had a "normal" looking vagina at one point in utero, *ergo* they are girls. In most cases, CAH girls grow up to identify as women (although at rates less than the general population). In other words, there is a widespread belief that the surgeries are justified because parents and surgeons believe that the CAH child (or any intersex child, really) can be safely placed into one side of the gender binary, and thus is not truly intersex. This betrays a profound and dangerous misunderstanding of what intersex is though.

A 2017 report by interACT: Advocates for Intersex Youth and Human Rights Watch entitled "'I Want to Be Like Nature Made Me': Medically Unnecessary Surgeries on Intersex Children in the US" presents a simple but effective definition of intersex. Although some contest the definition, it is still the most widely accepted. Intersex describes people born "with anatomies that are considered 'atypical' for either male or female bodies."[22] According to this definition, and really all the variations on this definition, CAH girls are intersex because they are born with a body that is atypical in terms of the strict standards. Now, to say that all of the markers except one are there, which means the ambiguous genitalia are just an anomaly, is ridiculous. The presence of a single intersex trait is what makes the person intersex. It really would not make much sense for surgeons to go around recommending cosmetic surgeries on the genitalia of non-intersex infants.

While other markers may be less ambiguous, and this may make it easier to predict the most likely gender identity of a child, it will always be nothing more than an educated guess. There will always be significant numbers of people who fall outside the prediction. This means that if we surgically affirm gender onto bodies of intersex infants, there will always be a group of people who reject the body they were given by doctors. The only sure way to avoid this is to let the individual decide for themselves if they want surgery.

We understand if parents do not want to identify their child as intersex, or that children born with an intersex condition may grow up and not identify as intersex. That is certainly their choice and their right, which we fully support. However, we reject the idea that one should refuse the label of intersex simply to justify medically unnecessary surgical interventions. Call the condition what you will, the name is not as important as the practice that it facilitates. If you feel your girl is a girl because she has two X chromosomes, so be it. That does not mean that you have the right to surgically alter her body, without her consent, to make her fit the girl mold. They are mutually exclusive issues. We have raised Rosie to be a girl, and we believe at this point that she will identify as a girl. But we let her lead the process of identification, we let her explore what that means for her body, her mind, and her interactions with others. In short, you can believe that your child is a girl or a boy, and you can raise them as such without imposing it upon them surgically.

The landscape of what it means to be a woman or a man is constantly shifting, which makes any claims to a definitive gender marker highly dubious. A good example of this is the case of Caster Semenya, the South African track and field sprinter who won Olympic gold in the 2016 summer games. Semenya has a condition called hyperandrogenism, which is simply a term to describe high levels of naturally occurring testosterone in women as a result of having internal testes. It should be noted that men are incapable of suffering from hyperandrogenism, as no level of testosterone is too high for a man. Semenya has had to endure unnecessary scrutiny and humiliatingly invasive inquiries due to her condition. For example, she has been subjected to sex verification tests, and she was briefly barred from competing until the results of sex tests were completed. Other racers have accused her of being a man, and argued that the competition is unfair if she is allowed to run. The International Association for Athletics Federations (IAAF) determined in 2011 that women with hyperandrogenism must either retire from competition, or take testosterone blockers to push their hormones back to below "male" levels. Other women were also subjected to genetic mapping, hormone testing, physical examinations, and so on, when regulators of the IAAF felt there was a need. Semenya identifies as a woman, she has two X chromosomes, she was raised as a girl, and has a vagina.[23] The goalposts are ever shifting in these debates, and there simply will never be a conclusive, definitive marker where we can say, "yes, this is a woman" or "this is a man" because these categories are socially constructed and built upon faulty premises. There is, and always has been, wide variation in our bodies, our sexuality, anatomy, and gender identity. The idea that there are two stable categories of male and female, and each corresponds to a set of characteristics that are also unchanging, is a mythology.

Judith Butler's landmark book *Gender Trouble* provides a useful breakdown of the contested relationship between gender, sexuality, and biology. Butler's theory rests on the idea of the Heterosexual Matrix, which is the historic connection between gender identity, which is to say how you perform your gender in either masculine or feminine ways; your sexuality, which is whether you like men or women as potential sexual partners; and biology, which is whether you have a penis or vagina, and other physical markers of one sex or the other (or both). The Matrix assumes stability in the binary of these categories, and suggests they are all naturally occurring.[24] In other words, if you have a penis, then naturally you would act in masculine ways (short hair, emotionally detached, prefer sports and hate pink, etc.), and you would be sexually attracted to the exact opposite: women with a vagina, who act feminine (long hair, love pink, prefer to talk and shop, etc.), and who like masculine men. For decades we have operated under this system, believing, or at least acting like we believe, that this is the "normal" and "natural" order of things. The crucial point about Butler's theory is that all the categories are related, and rely on the permanency of the others to make any sense. If any one of them is contested, the whole Matrix begins to unravel. When we start to see the presence of gay men in our society, for example, we can no longer assume a straightforward connection between a penis, masculinity, and attraction to women. Maybe the man has a penis, acts in traditionally masculine ways, but likes men who are the same as him. Maybe you are a woman who likes men, but rejects the frilly pink dresses associated with traditional femininity. We have always had these outliers to the Matrix, but have historically made excuses: "she's a tomboy," or "he's sensitive." In reality, we have always been forced to reconcile the fact that the categories are untrue and oversimplified.

Consider the shifting roles of men in society as well. More and more men are taking on childcare responsibilities, traditionally seen as the domain of women.

A Pew Research Study found that the amount of time that men spend on childcare has tripled since the 1960s, and nearly half of those men said that they feel they still spend too little time with their kids.[25] In this example, we have traditionally heterosexual men eagerly engaging in an activity that was considered too feminine only a generation ago. These shifts happen all the time, and they show that our system for understanding gender is flawed. When we start to introduce bisexual people, transgender people, and intersex people into the conversation (or many others), it becomes untenable for us to continue to argue that there is a firm, unchanging, direct connection between how we like to act, who we like to be intimate with, and how we were born. The variations are endless and complex. As such, we cannot continue to justify intersex infant genital surgeries based upon the Heterosexual Matrix, when we now know how unsound it actually is. This Matrix is what justifies surgery on intersex infants, because without it, there would be no rush to start making the body fit into these binary categories. If we start from the idea that all bodies are different, and it is impossible to predict the gender identity or sexual attractions of someone at birth, then it becomes a simple extension to say we have to wait and see how our kids grow before we attempt any irreversible procedures.

"We don't have any data on the risks of delaying surgery"

We call this the "Devil you know" argument for surgery, which is as dubious and slippery as the rest of them. Simply put, doctors would rather stick with the devil they know (surgery) than shift their policies towards delaying surgery because, they argue, the negative impact of delaying may in fact be worse. They have no way of knowing that delaying surgery will be better, and they cannot guarantee that it will not have even worse consequences. As a result, before any such change in policy can occur, doctors argue that they need solid evidence that to do so would not cause more harm than good. On the face, this seems like a reasonable position, but it too is fraught with problems.

First, doctors created the policy of conducting normalizing surgery on intersex genitals in infancy without any evidence to support it. Without the research of John Money, which has been unequivocally discredited, one has to wonder if these intersex surgeries would ever have become so common. If the medical establishment created a policy on treating intersex infants without data, certainly they can change it using the existing data, which is ample in its proof that these surgeries can have devastating effects for intersex individuals. Many sympathetic doctors continue to invoke some hypothetical group of patients who are happy with the surgeries conducted on them as infants, and use their existence as evidence that the surgeries are largely successful. We do not deny that many patients are happy with having had the surgeries as infants, and would not change anything about their care, but that is not an ethical justification, it is random chance. It is simply stating that the ends justify the means in a percentage of the cases. Doctors have it backwards when they say that they need data on outcomes for delaying surgery, while at the same time continuing to perform surgeries that they adopted without evidence, and for which clear data exists that proves these surgeries are causing significant harm to people. The Hippocratic Oath says, "First do no harm," not "First we need to see the data."

Second, the idea that delaying surgery has some potential negative consequences is really another way of concealing the heterosexist ideas of the doctors. When they say that they need data that proves delaying surgery won't cause harm, what they mean is that they believe that delaying surgery will cause emotional harm, and they want to see data that proves otherwise. This is a phenomenon known to researchers and scientists as confirmation bias; it describes the ways that people interpret new information in a manner that confirms their existing set of beliefs. For example, if you are a surgeon who believes that people will be happier if they have "normal" looking genitalia, then even when you are presented with evidence that these infant genital surgeries cause emotional suffering, you may be unmoved by the account. Some doctors argue that the stories of intersex activists represent a small fraction, and that there is a silent majority of patients who are happy with the surgeries conducted on them as children. Likewise, if you are a doctor who believes that children will be better off with a cosmetically "normal" anatomy, then you might insist on data that disproves your assumptions, even if you know that such a study is not possible. And even if it were possible, you might not believe it would matter anyways. The point is that many doctors and surgeons are ignoring the stories of intersex people who have suffered, ignoring the evidence, because they believe they are doing the right thing regardless, and are searching for ways to protect that belief.

Conclusion

What we have listed above are the types of justifications that doctors and surgeons have given for continuing to do genital surgeries on intersex infants. Some of the doctors in charge of Rosie's care gave us these explanations personally and, in other cases, we have encountered these justifications during our advocacy work, speaking with other parents or debating with medical professionals about the practice. In all the instances, when subjected to interrogation or evidence, the justifications fall apart. Surgeons and supporters of surgery betray longstanding biases regarding gender, sexuality, and anatomy, and fail to take into account the mountain of shifting perspectives and evidence that contradicts the biases.

We believe in most cases that these doctors are acting with the best interests of their patients in mind, which is all the more reason for them to reevaluate the common practices to ensure they are not causing harm, and that they stand up to interrogation. No doctor can say that they believe fully that the practice of cosmetically altering the genitals of an intersex child, without their consent, is still the best course of action; not when so many stories exist that contradict that claim. If you are a doctor, consider these arguments and the lack of evidence to support them. If you are a parent of an intersex child, and your child's doctor uses these arguments to convince you to consent to surgery, do not be afraid to challenge them.

CHAPTER 4

Waiting is Easy

In the previous chapter, we discussed the justifications typically used for surgery, and explained why they should be rejected by parents of intersex children, or anyone in a position to influence policies about infant intersex genital surgery. In this chapter, we would like to do two things. First, we would like to provide readers with the positive justifications for delaying surgery. So rather than focusing exclusively on what doctors and surgeons argue are the reasons for surgery, in this chapter we would like to illuminate the positive outcomes that are possible by delaying surgery. Second, we would like to focus on some of the challenges that may arise while raising a surgery-free intersex child, and provide strategies for overcoming those challenges. It is our hope, of course, that people who have an intersex child will not consent to surgery, and we would like to help give them the confidence to deal with their specific sets of challenges that come with raising an intersex child.

Much of the discourse on intersex infant genital surgery focuses on the harm that may result from unwanted, non-consensual procedures. Indeed, this is of the utmost importance, and it is why we devoted the previous chapter to that topic. Proponents of surgery have repeatedly contended that, while surgery has potential drawbacks for a percentage of the children subjected to it, there is no way of knowing that the alternative is any better. In other words, surgery may be bad they say, but delaying surgery could be worse. Moreover, because they do not know what will happen if they stop the surgeries, continuing to perform them persists as the just option. This is logically absurd, as absence of evidence is not evidence of absence. To put it another way, just because no systematic scientific studies have been conducted that prove that delaying surgeries causes less harm than infant surgeries, that does not prove that the original practice is justified. Let us not forget that there is evidence that these surgeries cause harm, mountains of evidence in fact, which should be enough to end the practice immediately. Moreover, there is no evidence to support continued surgeries, either. However, it is worth exploring the benefits of delaying surgery so that any lingering doubts about the right choice can safely be put to rest.

What is to be gained by waiting?

When the urological surgeon, Dr. Dukat, recommended operating on Rosie so that she would grow up not knowing that her body was ever different, he believed he was going to convince us to approve the surgery, when all it did was reinforce the fact that we would be making a huge mistake by consenting to any procedure. We had quite the opposite desire to the doctor, it seemed. We *wanted* Rosie to know that she was born this way, and that many people are born with variations in their bodies, and this variety is what makes us all beautiful in our own ways. Rosie will grow up knowing that she was born with an intersex body, but loved unconditionally nonetheless, and empowered to explore the world confident in her distinctiveness. One of the major concerns that we had was that we would be extinguishing this perspective from her personal history. How are we to know the ways that growing up intersex could positively impact not only her life, but the lives of people around her? It could end up being a vital part of how she sees herself, sees others, and views the world at large: through the lens of a beautiful and unique intersex body. What if leaving her body intact led her to explore a career in medicine, focused on treating patients like her, or led her to write a novel about a child with an intersex condition? What if growing up this way inspired her to direct a film, write music, or make art that tells her story? How could we know that she won't pursue a career in politics, seeking expanded social justice for LGBTQI+ people? The world may be changed for the better by the presence of people who view themselves and society in ways that are drastically different to the rest of the population. Rosie's surgeon shared a fear that many other supporters of these surgeries have, which is that psychological damage is somehow inevitable if the intersex child is ever to see themselves as different. This message is simple: different is bad. We disagree. We are all different in many ways, and those differences are what make us wonderful, beautiful, and awesome.

Researchers who study the ethics of LGBTQI+ issues expressed concerns about the dangers of over-medicalization of sexuality long ago. According to Timothy F. Murphy in his book *Gay Science: The Ethics of Sexual Orientation Research* (1997), a central debate in this field revolves around how scientific research on LGBTQI+ issues might be deployed. For example, some believe that it could be used against gay and lesbian people. If research was to uncover a gene or hereditary marker that reliably predicted a gay or lesbian child, then parents might opt to abort them. Or, worse, politicians in authoritarian states hostile to gays and lesbians may force abortions on parents pregnant with children positive for the markers. Even in democratic states, an objective scientific indicator of being gay could be used to discriminate or persecute. According to Murphy, it is not hard to see how the medicalization of sexual attraction could easily lead to an overall reduction in the number of gay people in our population. Conversely, Murphy identifies groups of commentators who feel that scientific research into the nature of same-sex attraction could potentially eliminate the moralistic persecutions that plague gay and lesbian populations around the world. If irrefutable scientific proof emerged that shows that being gay is naturally occurring in our population, and not tied to the morality of choices, then it becomes easier to extend full social, legal, and cultural protections to gay people. For intersex people, the latter concerns are not relevant since everyone agrees that to be intersex means you have a naturally occurring, congenital medical condition. However, the so-called treatment is very much embedded with the same ethical concerns as Murphy describes above. The apparent absence of intersex people in our society is likely due to the fact that they rarely have a chance to identify as such because they are medically altered as infants, or forced to live with such a high degree of shame and stigma that they are reluctant to ever identify themselves as intersex.

Leaving our children intact helps spread the word throughout society that there is no ideal male or female standard body; no perfect, no "normal" way of being human; and that we are all free to explore and determine for ourselves who we are and what we want to be. Intersex conditions, while technically physical, are only "problems" because we have a culture and society that views these bodies as abnormal. The medical research has shown repeatedly that these physical manifestations of intersex conditions only rarely present symptoms that are dangerous. Rosie, for example, has CAH, which must be managed with constant monitoring of steroid levels. Surgery would not change that. She would always need to be treated for her endocrine disorder regardless of her unique genitalia. So there is a medical necessity in treating her CAH, but her genitalia are separate in that they have no medically pressing reason to be altered. Rather, her ambiguous genitalia are part of a social problem, not a physical one. Once we can put it in these terms, it becomes easier to see that the solution to this is not to surgically "correct" her body, further perpetuating the social conditions that give rise to the "problem" in the first place, but rejecting that approach altogether. We have to embrace differences in bodies. The correction should not be surgically "normalizing" her genitalia, but correcting the belief that she has something wrong with her by normalizing her body as it exists.

As we have said repeatedly, we are not anti-surgery so much as we are pro-consent. If the time arrives when Rosie decides that she wants to have a surgery and live a private, quiet life with no explicit connection between her condition and public life, that is her choice and we will support it enthusiastically. The point is that it has to be her choice, her decision, and only hers. Our responsibility as parents is to preserve that right for her so that, when the time comes, she can make the decision on her own. Truly, this is not a controversial position to take. We do this with our children in most cases. It is not hard to see how arranging the future of your child when they are just born could be fraught with mistakes, even if the intentions are good. How many of us would be completely comfortable arranging the marriage of our newborns in this day and age, knowing very well that we have no way of knowing if our child will be gay or straight, or asexual?

There is an underlying assumption about intersex people whose bodies are left intact, which proponents of surgery appear to hold, but which is never spoken. It is a deeply heterosexist assumption that any body that does not strictly conform to traditional heterosexual standards is revolting, and that the person will forever be sexually undesirable to potential partners if they are not surgically normalized. In this way, we can understand why so many doctors and parents believe they are acting in the best interest of the child, but this assumption is without a basis in fact. Again, what we *do* have evidence for is that intersex people who have a history of surgery, lies, stigma, and shame, struggle with intimacy as a result of those repeated traumas.[1] It is foolish to believe that heterosexual male partners will be horrified by a woman's enlarged clitoris, especially since there is no evidence to support this. It is especially dubious when surgeons use that assumption to justify cosmetic surgeries on those girls, which has the potential to traumatize them so much that they struggle with intimacy, all based on speculative anecdotal evidence. As a society, it seems we would rather have women who are unable to feel confident and comfortable with their bodies, than have men who are uncomfortable seeing a slightly enlarged clitoris. Related to this argument is the idea that intersex children left intact, especially young girls, will grow to hate themselves because of their bodily differences. We live in a culture and a society that values beauty, and punishes difference, so the logic suggests that we eliminate as many potential markers of difference as possible. Many people will say that they may not like it, but this is the way it is. But, we ask, where does it end? As we argued in previous chapters, teaching your child to love themselves unconditionally has the potential to instill the confidence within them that will allow them to weather any future storm. Trying to stamp out differences so that a child will not be singled out for negative attention is futile; we will always have differences and people will always identify them, for good or bad. So a better approach is to try to foreground differences, celebrate them all, and teach our children to do the same, so that we may finally neutralize the tyranny of "normality."

We argue that if more people leave their intersex children intact into adulthood, aside from ensuring they raise people who feel empowered and respected to make decisions about their own body, we may also greatly increase the likelihood that future adults will encounter an unaltered intersex body, and a strong, confident, unashamed intersex person. As more and more adults come into contact with other adults with intersex bodies, who are unashamed and confident, the stigma that drives these surgeries will die away.

How to raise an intersex child

One of the questions that we get asked the most while discussing Rosie is, "what's her day to day life like?" Journalists have asked us repeatedly how her intersex condition is managed, and our answer is always the same: right now, it's a complete non-issue. We keep waiting for one of the problems that surgeons and pro-surgery parents have warned us about to appear, but they never do. Parents of intersex children wondering what will happen if they delay surgery should take some comfort in the fact that the only issues we have had with her body have been minor and easily remedied. Frankly, they are issues that are not all that dissimilar or uncommon from what non-intersex children occasionally have to deal with. Rosie has never had a urinary tract infection (UTI), even though we were led to believe that these infections would be frequent if we did not do surgery. Occasionally, Rosie can experience irritation that comes from the general attitude towards hygiene of a child her age, not unlike that which is experienced by uncircumcised boys. This may require, at most, a bit of extra cleaning and the application of a topical, over-the-counter skin cream. Jeans have been known to bother her, especially in hot weather, but this too is moderate and infrequent. She chooses to wear skirts, dresses, and leggings. To be fair, our son also complains about his genitals being "sticky" while wearing jeans in the hot weather, a problem that is common for boys, and not a justifiable reason to consider surgery.

Rosie is in school all day now, and has been attending day-care facilities or half-day preschool since she was two years old. In those early days, she had a variety of day-care teachers change her diapers, without shock or horror, without so much as a casual mention of it to us, in fact. When she was still in diapers, we would often come to pick her up from day-care only to find the children's semi-communal bathroom filled with half-naked children in various stages of cleaning themselves. The point is, as many people have seen Rosie's body as have seen any other child that age, and it has never been a shameful, traumatic, or uncomfortable situation. Prior to sending her to any of these facilities, we would typically let the staff know about her body so that they were not surprised or blindsided if there were to be an incident and, without exception, all acted professionally when told. This is precisely what one would expect to happen.

Now that she is more autonomous, she uses the bathroom at school on her own, in private, as the rest of us do. She has more control over who sees her body, and employs age-appropriate measures to protect her own privacy. (Like all five-year-olds, she occasionally likes to show her naked butt to whoever is in the vicinity.) Of course, this is what we expect from a child who has no shame in her body, and likes to emulate her siblings, who likewise feel comfortable in acting in similar ways.

She does not require a special bathroom, or any special arrangements whatsoever. I doubt that even if we had not informed her teachers about her body, there would ever be an opportunity for her condition to come to light.

Another question we get is about the inevitable future sleep-over, swimming pool party, or locker room encounter, where Rosie will have to expose her body. To this, we have two answers. First, she has already gone to play in pools and sandboxes with her friends, without incident. She is young, of course, and her friends are, too, so at this point we would not expect them to be as cruel as adolescents can be. But, again, by the time she reaches the age where she is more likely to encounter unkindness related to her body, she will not know that there is anything which she is supposed to be ashamed of. She will be able to think back, and remember all the times people saw her body and did not care, and she will take comfort in the fact that her parents and family have loved and respected her body for her whole life. Rather than dreading some terrible future encounter where her secret is exposed, an event that may never actually happen, we hope to empower her to enjoy her life, her body, and her friends as anyone else would. As we said in previous chapters, you cannot stop other children from bullying, but you can diminish the negative impact it has on your child by creating a safe, welcoming, place for them to grow, learn, and be loved.

There are stories from adults with intersex conditions, many of them with CAH and closely affiliated with the CARES Foundation, who argue that they are glad that their parents consented to surgery on them when they were babies. Some of their stories simply repeat what their parents and doctors had told them was the reason for having the surgery, but are based on hypotheticals. A *Washington Post* article from October of 2017 by Nora Caplan-Bricker[2] quotes several people affiliated with the CARES Foundation. One such person said that if her parents had been prevented from consenting to her surgery in infancy, she would have struggled to explain missing school to classmates when she eventually got the surgery as a teenager. This works on the assumption that a CAH person is going to want a surgery, which in her case she did, but not every child does. Second, and more importantly, this reproduces the stigma that there is something shameful or strange about her condition, that she must conceal her intersex traits from her peers because they will bully her, or embarrass her. This is the same line of reasoning articulated by Karen Su, an endocrinologist at Weill Cornell Medicine, and the CARES Foundation medical director, who is quoted in the same article as saying that if you wait until the children turn into adolescents before doing the surgery, then you open them up to potential embarrassment at wearing bathing suits, leotards, or going into dressing rooms. Even if this is true, which there is no evidence for, since when does avoiding embarrassment justify cosmetic surgeries on children too young to consent? The adults who had surgery as infants and support the practice all seem to believe that they were spared some hypothetical exposure they are convinced would have been more traumatic than the surgery. We wonder if they were ever bullied or made fun of for anything else, not related to being born with an intersex condition. Were they ever made to feel embarrassed? Obviously, being occasionally uncomfortable is a part of growing up. The solution to this is for parents to raise children who are empathetic to other children, and who have developed high self-esteem capable of managing the occasional bully or embarrassing interaction.

The pro-surgery faction has created this mythology of embarrassment, and use it both to convince parents to have surgery by claiming they want to prevent embarrassment, and as justification for surgeries after-the-fact ("I'm so glad I was spared the embarrassment of my friends seeing my body"). How do they know this is a traumatically humiliating experience when they were spared from ever living through it? In fact, since more than 80 percent of intersex children are cosmetically altered in infancy, there's almost no one that has lived through it.[3] There appears to be a misplaced anxiety by the pro-surgery advocates that the worst possible thing that can happen to a child is for them to be mistaken for someone of the opposite gender, or for a boy to have to urinate sitting down, or for a girl to have to explain that they were born with a clitoris that is larger than the average, or some other social encounter such as this. Pro-surgery advocates believe these possibilities to be so potentially traumatic, so damaging, that they will openly support cosmetic surgeries on infants who cannot consent, even though we know beyond a shadow of a doubt that the trauma associated with doing the surgeries is very real for a significant percentage of the people.

We can think of at least a few of examples where mistakes have unintended, positive outcomes for a small group of people, while having very serious negative outcomes for others. Solidifying that mistake as policy is a dangerous proposition though. Pro-surgery advocates in the CARES Foundation argue that since most intersex girls with CAH identify as girls and want a surgery later on, this justifies doing the surgery in infancy (even though some will reject it later, and they acknowledge this). This is a clear example of the tyranny of the majority, whereby the larger proportion of intersex adults may be happy to have had a surgery because they feel they would have been embarrassed by their intact body, and so a blanket policy of operating on all intersex people during infancy becomes the norm, even though a significant proportion, albeit a minority, are subject to a practice that does them great physical and emotional harm as they grow.

Does raising an intersex child mean raising a gender-neutral child?

This question is also fair, especially for people who have had very little interactions with literature on gender, sexuality, and intersex conditions. The answer though is a straightforward "no," you do not have to raise your child as gender-neutral in order to raise them as intersex. A famous quote by the renowned drag queen RuPaul, which appeared in his autobiography, and also hangs in bright red letters on the wall of the Museum of Modern Art in New York City, says, "You're born naked, and the rest is drag." What RuPaul means with this wonderful turn of phrase is that all of us put on a show where we perform our gender using a variety of markers and signs that communicate to others what our gender identity is, and by extension what our assumed biology and sexuality are. Having long hair, wearing pink, wearing make-up, swishing your hips when you walk, and the like, are all external markers of femininity. Conversely, short hair, muscles, suits and ties, and the color blue, are all associated with masculinity. When children are born, their genitalia are inspected, and expectations about their gender and sexuality are communicated based on their body, using the above-mentioned markers. They are taught how to perform as either masculine or feminine. For example, girls are given dolls to foster a maternal "instinct," they're allowed to grow their hair, and encouraged to wear pink. Boys are given trucks or guns to play with, their hair is kept short so they are not mistaken for girls, and they are taught to be tough and urinate standing up. These conventions are socially taught. Boys and girls learn to perform these tasks, and many others, convincingly through socialization, so that eventually it becomes automatic.

There are many problematic aspects to raising kids in this environment. Encouraging boys to always be tough, to avoid associating with feminine things, to hide emotions, and to expect female attention, has had disastrous outcomes in our society. Generations of men have been raised who are prone to loneliness, isolation, and violence, the negative effects of which are disproportionately experienced by women. But it would be very difficult, if not impossible, for everyone to raise their children in a gender-neutral way. Many people enjoy identifying with one gender or another, or both, or neither. Some people, like RuPaul, love to toy with and experiment with gender performance, and people should have the right to exist in this world in the way they feel most comfortable.

That being said, our perspective on raising an intersex child is not to raise Rosie as gender-neutral, but to raise her as a girl until such time as she can decide for herself what type of gender identity best fits her, and then to show support for whatever she decides. In this regard, we take the same approach with Rosie as we do with Silas, our older son. He identifies as a boy, he dresses like one, and uses male pronouns. If, at some point, he decides that he no longer is comfortable identifying this way, then we would support his decision. For the time being, we assume that our children are statistically more likely to identify with the gender we assigned them, and so we proceed under that assumption. To put it simply, you do not have to raise an intersex child as gender-neutral, you just have to be willing to accept that the gender you assigned them may change, and you have to be open and supportive of that. And in the case of intersex children, if their gender identity does not change, then they can lead the process of affirming their identity, which may or may not include surgery.

It is in our collective best interest to try to soften the strict gender binaries that plague our society though, and this need not strictly apply to how we raise intersex children.

With Silas and Rosie, we have tried to encourage them to think about their identity as not being stringently dictated by their gender preferences. When Silas wants to experiment with clothes and make-up, he is allowed and encouraged to do so. We inspire him to express his emotions, to seek out affectionate contact with the people he loves, and to explore behaviors otherwise deemed unacceptable for young boys. Rosie, too, is encouraged to engage in similar activities that challenge conventional gender norms, and not because she is intersex, but because we feel she will be happier if she is allowed to determine her own path and identity. Children of any sex or gender should be taught that it is okay to express emotions, not just little girls. Likewise, we should not teach only our little boys to speak their mind in public and to be assertive. The desires of most parents to simply raise children who are not constrained by society's gendered expectations is understandable, and applies to intersex children as well as non-intersex children.

Being intersex is something we want Rosie to understand fully. Many of the intersex adults we have met have told us that they learned they were intersex in their teen years, or later, and that in several cases their parents and doctors knew the whole time, but said nothing. Many of these people felt the emotional trauma associated with being lied to, or misled, by parents and doctors had been nearly as damaging psychologically as the surgeries were. We did not want that to be the case for Rosie, and a friend of the family (more family than friend) named Jay Lowery offered us some advice. Jay and his wife Linsey had just recently adopted a daughter they named Eloise, and when asked when and how they planned to tell her about the adoption, they said that they intended to continually make Eloise's adoption an integral part of the story they tell her about herself. In a similar way, suddenly finding out that you are adopted can be frightening or confusing, and can lead to anger and mistrust. Our friends said that they give Eloise age-appropriate information about her birth mother, who they keep in contact with, and about the process they undertook to bring her into the family. As she grows and has more questions, they said, the plan is to be open and truthful so that the adoption continues to be something Eloise understands completely as she matures. This, we felt, was analogous to our own situation. As Rosie grows and has more questions, we plan to explain her body differences to her in ways she can understand, and feel good about. Rosie knows she is intersex, but she does not yet know that her genitalia look different than other girls, just that all bodies are different from one another, and that is not a bad thing. The time will come when she has more specific questions about her own body, and at that point she will receive the answers she seeks in a straightforward and honest way. How can we expect her to be able to decide on her own if she wants a surgery if we fail to give her the tools and language to be fully comfortable in her own skin as it currently exists?

Related to this, we also use anatomically correct language when describing Rosie's body to her, and also in discussing other bodies around her. This strategy has proved to be one of the most significant, but overlooked, steps a family can take to raise children who are comfortable with varieties in gender identity (not just for parents raising an intersex child). There is a propensity for parents and caregivers to use silly juvenile euphemisms to describe genitals to children, out of embarrassment or habit, but this can have seriously dangerous downstream effects. Creating shame or stigma around a word increases shame about the thing itself. So calling your child's vulva a "woo-hoo" or calling a penis a "wee-wee" makes them embarrassed when people discuss these body parts. They learn to feel like they do not understand their own body, that they have no ownership over their genitals because they do not have knowledge of them. These body parts are not to be taken seriously, or understood fully, but instead denote something comical, silly, or taboo. Again, this is an easy problem to remedy. Get into the habit of referring to your children's bodies using the actual anatomical words that describe them, and give them as much information as they can appropriately handle based upon their questions and inquiries. This proves much more difficult for parents than it does for kids, the latter being much more receptive to adult conversations about anatomy than we give them credit for.

With Rosie, we refer to her enlarged clitoris as a phallus, and have told her what a clitoris is for. Our son has also been aware since he was very little that his penis was referred to as such. There are two things we learned from this exercise. One is that knowledge of the terms creates comfort with the concepts. Rosie, for example, knows that babies grow in a uterus, and are delivered through the vaginal canal. When she was exposed to a friend at school who said "babies grow in our tummies," she corrected them by explaining how the uterus functions, and that the uterus is different to our stomachs. To her, this seemed like an obvious difference that everyone should want to know about. Her friends were simply uninformed. She had no discomfort explaining what a vagina is, or how a baby is delivered through it. A related benefit to this is that her comfort with the knowledge of her body means that she can easily and comfortably articulate any problems she may have with her genitals. Even though she has never had a UTI, if she did experience any discomfort, she would not feel shy about telling us about it, and would be able to differentiate the nature of her problem. We have already reaped the benefits of this approach when Rosie has experienced an irritated phallus, and asked for a cream to relieve the irritation. She was comfortable asking for help, and was able to easily explain where the irritation was occurring.

Second, comfort with the knowledge of her body, and other bodies, makes it much easier for us to discuss variations that are naturally occurring in our population so as to reduce the stigma. As a result, we use those differences to make her more comfortable with her own intersex body. Reducing or eliminating the shame associated with having an intersex body is a far easier task when Rosie can fully understand the things about her body that make it intersex. We want Rosie to know that her body is different, and to understand exactly how it is different, so that we can situate that explanation in a larger context that says that all bodies are different in some ways, and that these differences are all part of being human. Many adults give young children very little credit for their ability to understand and talk about issues for which we believe they lack the maturity to understand. The reality is, of course, that we are uncomfortable with the topic, and we assume that our kids must also be, so we create euphemisms and convolutions that allow us to sidestep straightforward discussions that make us squirmy.

Using correct language is a small, but important step in eliminating the stigma for intersex people. Ask yourself how many four-year-old children could explain what testicles are for, or know how a baby is grown and delivered. The answer is probably very few, not because they cannot understand these things, but because they have been kept from obtaining correct, destigmatized information about their own bodies.

Taking away Rosie's privacy

The criticism that we most often get regarding our advocacy on behalf of intersex kids is a fair one. People have questioned if it is not hypocritical of us to argue that we want Rosie to have a role in whether she has surgery, and to put her out there in the public spotlight, but ignore the fact that she is too young to consent to having her business made public by us. Without exception, this has been our single biggest concern, at least after deciding against surgery. After all, we have agreed to participate in documentaries and newspaper interviews, and sit on various boards and committees, all the while openly discussing Rosie's private medical condition. We have reconciled this apparent contradiction, but it was not easy.

We asked Georgiann Davis, professor of Sociology at UNLV and intersex activist, for her advice on this topic before embarking on a public advocacy platform, and her counsel was incredibly helpful. A few days before the documentary film crew was set to arrive with Katie Couric, we called Georgiann to ask if she felt we were making a mistake by putting Rosie in front of the cameras. At that point, we were not planning to show Rosie's face in any of the footage. But we felt uncomfortable about this decision, and did not yet understand why.

"If this were any other medical condition," Georgiann said, "parents would not think twice about discussing it with the media if they thought it could help other people." This bit of wisdom fell on us like a hammer. In our attempt to remove the stigma associated with raising intersex children, we had fallen victim to the same thinking that treats intersex conditions as something shameful that must be hidden. She went on to explain her thinking using a popular example at the time: Batkid. In November, 2013, the Make-a-Wish Foundation staged an elaborate project to give a young cancer survivor, five-year-old Miles Scott, a Batman themed superhero day. Officials from all over the city of San Francisco pitched in to help stage the event, including the police department, the mayor, city councilors, and local news channels. It was the Make-a-Wish Foundation's biggest project ever, up to that point. Miles Scott received a video message from President Barack Obama, was given an official FBI "raid" jacket, a key to the city of San Francisco, and was cheered on by thousands of onlookers, who lined the streets to watch. This story was covered widely by the press inside and outside the United States, appearing on national, international, and local news outlets. The accompanying ten-minute video produced by the Make-a-Wish Foundation went viral, generating over one million views. There is even a documentary about the event, called *Batkid Begins*, which was released in 2015.

"I don't remember hearing in any of those news stories about Batkid that maybe those parents were making a mistake by showing that child's face all over the world. No one is discussing whether Batkid's private medical business is being jeopardized by that event. It's just a heartwarming story, and that's it. To me, this illustrates perfectly the problem. Cancer is not something people are generally ashamed of, it is not something that people hide. If we're not concerned with his privacy surrounding his cancer, then why should you be concerned about showing Rosie's face and discussing her medical history? After all, if you're not ashamed of her, and I know you're not, then there's nothing to hide."

If we are not ashamed of her, then there is nothing to hide. The veracity of this statement drastically changed our views on how to advocate for Rosie. Georgiann was right: we were not ashamed of Rosie, in fact we were and are incredibly proud of her, as we are of all our children. There did not seem to be a way to justify hiding her from the world when we would never have considered doing so with our children in order to raise awareness for a different type of condition. If Rosie had diabetes, for example, we would have jumped at the chance to put her out into the world in order to help raise awareness of that condition. It never would have even crossed our minds that she may one day resent this choice, or that other parents of children with diabetes would be angry with our choice.

One problem remained though. It is possible, and perhaps likely even, that Rosie will grow up and enter the awful teenage years (no parent has yet figured out how to fast-forward these years), and she will come to us demanding to know why we did not consent to surgery, or why we put her private business out into the world without a single thought for how it might affect her later in life. We raised this issue with Georgiann, and she again assuaged our fears with an idea that we found very comforting.

"There's no way to predict what a teenager is going to be upset about," Georgiann said. This is sage advice. We know from raising teenagers that things that we think are unimportant or fleeting concerns are crucial to teenagers. Attempting to raise a child, while keeping an eye on what the future teenager will be angry about, is an exercise in futility. Still, Georgiann said, there was a way to help Rosie be more comfortable with both our decision to delay surgery, and our public advocacy.

"For many intersex adults, especially those who had surgeries and had parents and doctors lie to them, the biggest issue is that no one gave any thought to what we wanted or how we might feel when we get older, or about how their choices might affect us later on down the road. The fact that you are coming to me with these concerns and questions shows that you are always considering the impact of your choices on Rosie, and that should make you feel a bit better." It truly did make us feel less guilty about agreeing to appear in the documentary, at the very least. Most parents give very little thought to what their children are going to be interested in, or angry about, when they reach adolescence, simply because there is no possible way to accurately predict those circumstances so far in advance.

And then, Georgiann gave us an idea that we never would have thought of in a million years. "A way for you to show Rosie that you did consider her feelings, that you were thinking about how she might be impacted by your decisions, would be for you to write a letter to her now that she can open when she is mature enough." This seemed to us to be a stroke of brilliance. The mere fact that we took the time to write a letter a decade in advance would serve as irrefutable evidence that we did contemplate the ramifications of our choices on Rosie's future and, although she may not agree with our decisions, she will at the very least be able to understand why we made the choices we made. We talked a lot about whether we should share the letter we wrote in this book, but ultimately decided that we would keep it private. That is just for our Rosebud.

CHAPTER 5

The Future of Intersex Children

As we write this book, there is a palpable shift in the United States over the surgery paradigm for intersex children. Many in the intersex community believe that the tide is beginning to turn against surgeries. A group called Physicians for Human Rights released a statement saying that they were "deeply alarmed by the fact that [intersex children] are often subjected to irreversible medically unnecessary surgeries...before they are able to provide informed consent."[1] In a surprising move, the North American Society for Pediatric and Adolescent Gynecology (NASPAG) released their own statement recommending that any surgical interventions on intersex children be delayed if it is safe to do so, in order to allow time for the child to develop their own gender identity, and nurture the capacity to actively participate in any decisions regarding surgeries. Even more encouraging is the fact that the Pediatric Endocrine Society signed onto that NASPAG statement, fully endorsing delayed surgical interventions for the first time.[2] The American Medical Student Association also has asked that medical school education be amended to include mandatory "training on intersex health such that children born as intersex are afforded bodily autonomy and self-determination."[3] The two most important medical associations in terms of their ability to end these surgeries, the American Medical Association and the Societies for Pediatric Urology, have been disappointing in their responses. The latter has been exceptionally obdurate regarding their standards for treating intersex children, even releasing a statement in 2017 affirming their belief that surgeries on intersex children are justifiable.[4]

For the second year in a row, the US State Department affirmed its commitment to intersex rights by stating, "At a young age, intersex persons routinely face forced medical surgeries without free or informed consent. These interventions jeopardize their physical integrity and ability to live freely."[5] Chase Strangio, a staff lawyer with the American Civil Liberties Union working on LGBTQI+ issues, published a statement on the organization's website saying:

> It is plainly unethical, cruel, and unnecessary to perform surgeries on the genitals of children and infants because we are afraid that their bodies do not seem normal and out of an impulse to "assign" a binary sex to a child before that child can articulate their gender. We must do better than that.[6]

The list of organizations, both governmental and private, that are recognizing the dangers associated with these surgeries is steadily increasing, which is encouraging. But we believe it would be a mistake to assume that, at this point, we are on an inexorable path towards bodily autonomy for intersex children. There is much more to do, and if the statement by the Societies for Pediatric Urology is any indication, the possibility that these surgeries will continue is still very real. We would like to put forward two broad recommendations, which are obviously not exhaustive, but can serve as a roadmap for how to move towards reconciliation with the medical community.

Recognition

Arguably, one of the most significant hurdles facing the intersex community is that society does not fully understand what makes someone intersex, or what types of struggles they face. The medical establishment could play a much more significant role in rectifying this by helping to raise awareness about the issues facing intersex people. We would like to first call on the remaining medical associations to release statements in support of bodily autonomy and self-determination for intersex children, and to sponsor resolutions at their various professional organizations that support this position. At the very least, a moratorium on all cosmetic surgical procedures for intersex children should immediately be instated. Serious, honest debates have to begin to happen within the walls of the medical establishment in order to drive the types of change the intersex community has been waiting for, and those debates absolutely must include members of the intersex community harmed by these practices. Passing resolutions that officially affirm bodily autonomy for intersex children is the very least that can be done because it can draw attention to the historical trauma these people have experienced.

Related to this, we feel it would be an important step in the healing process for medical associations, especially those with a history of treating intersex patients, to recognize and address the trauma their standards of practice have inflicted on intersex people. This step is hard, we acknowledge, but is essential to our ability to move forward together in constructive ways. In our case, Rosie was spared any unnecessary medical intervention, so we consider ourselves quite fortunate. In spite of this, we still harbor a deep mistrust of the medical establishment because of its failure to work with us regarding Rosie's condition. We were pressured, misled, and bullied. We were given inadequate information, with no one to turn to within the hospital community for help. We had to seek out factual information about intersex issues, as well as support, completely on our own, at a time when we were at our most vulnerable.

It illuminated for us just how widespread this dangerous paradigm was, how many intersex children were being subjected to unnecessary surgery, how many parents were being pressured, misled, or outright bullied into consenting to a procedure that doctors have long known was controversial, and lacking in evidentiary support. Now think of the thousands of intersex adults who are currently struggling as a result of their trauma, who have deep physical and emotional scars left behind from their interactions with medical professionals over the years. Or think of the children who have had a surgery, but are still too young to fully comprehend what was done to them. What are we going to tell them when they start to articulate their own trauma, and we are forced to acknowledge then that we knew that surgery carried incredible risk? When you contemplate all these examples, our experience is innocuous by comparison.

The severity of the damage done to intersex people and their families varies, and none of it can be healed until intersex people can start to have their experiences validated, and their trauma acknowledged by the people who, regardless of intentions, were directly and indirectly responsible. We cannot overstate how important this step is as a starting point. It is impossible to proceed so long as medical practitioners continue to skirt responsibility and shift blame, at once validating and invalidating the damage done to intersex people by well-meaning medical personnel.

Responsible practices

The second recommendation is for the medical establishment to adopt a standard of care for treating intersex children that protects their bodily autonomy, their right to self-determination, and commits to first doing no harm. This is perhaps the easiest step, far easier than admitting mistakes, since there already exists a standard of care that addresses similar concerns for children who identify as transgender. The World Professional Association for Transgender Health (WPATH) has published an extensive standard of care document to be used in treating adults and adolescents with gender non-conforming identities.[7] One of the major issues is that medical providers (and some parents) have been remiss to associate conditions like Congenital Adrenal Hyperplasia with intersex or gender non-binary politics, which has meant that certain medical conditions have been treated outside of the established medical paradigms dealing with gender. This is a dangerous precedent, based upon a technicality, and it must be addressed. As it stands, intersex children are being treated in ways that drastically diverge from how non-intersex patients are treated.

It would be all too easy for the medical professionals that treat intersex children to adopt the WPATH standards, as this would have overwhelmingly positive outcomes for intersex children. These standards are well respected because they were instituted with the input from transgender people, unlike the current model practiced on intersex people. When discussing physical interventions on trans youth, the WPATH model recommends that "[b]efore any physical interventions are considered for adolescents, extensive exploration of psychological, family, and social issues should be undertaken." Treating patients who are potentially suffering from gender dysphoria begins with psychological interventions first, followed by reversible physical and social interventions, and then irreversible interventions only after the child has reached the age of 18, and can fully understand and consent to procedures.[8] The same standard should be extended to intersex people, whereby no irreversible physical interventions should happen until after that child and their family have been able to receive psychological care from a professional, and the child has reached an age of maturity where they can fully comprehend and consent to irreversible medical and surgical interventions. Otherwise, we are denying them the right to bodily autonomy enshrined in the WPATH standard, a right extended to all other non-intersex children.

A glaring contradiction between standards of care has emerged. How is it that the pediatric urologists are lacking in research outcomes that support delaying physical interventions on intersex children, but the WPATH, using the same lack of research, were able to draw a different set of conclusions about the justification for surgical interventions? The problem that these surgeons must face is that, for some issues, there will never be, and could never be, research that supports or refutes this particular issue unequivocally. And when that happens, when evidentiary research is not possible, we have no choice but to use assumptions. The cardinal assumption for all doctors is to first do no harm, and this is why the WPATH standard makes sense, because where evidence is lacking, the organization errs on the side of limiting interventions to that which first does no harm, and delays irreversible procedures till the patient is able to participate in the process. This is all that intersex activists have been asking for.

The physicians still clinging to the surgery model have contended that some parents of intersex children insist on surgery, so they [the doctors] feel intense pressure to perform them! This reconfiguring of the surgeons as the victim is absurdly laughable. But again, the WPATH standard addresses this, by pointing out that some parents of trans children may be against any type of transition for their kids, and may even insist on their children displaying the gender assigned to them at birth. This does not mean that we leave them to suffer in that environment though. In these cases, medical professionals are urged to arrange counseling to the family so that they can meet the emotional needs of that child, and support that child's gender identity in healthy ways. Difficult parents are nothing new, but the physician's first obligation is to the health and well-being of the patient, not the misguided opinions of the parent. While the latter can certainly present tremendous challenges to a doctor, those challenges do not absolve doctors of their duty to put the well-being of the patient above all else.

The argument that those of us advocating for an end to these surgeries have a radical position, is without merit. All that we are asking is that intersex children be treated the same way that non-intersex children are treated. Medical interventions for people presenting ambiguities between their gender identity and their body must start with psychological care, followed by reversible interventions, and finally irreversible interventions only after the child is able to give informed consent. Failure to treat intersex children in the same way is unethical and an injustice.

The final recommendation we present applies to anyone who wishes to make the world a better place for intersex people. We must all oppose discriminatory policies that target people based upon gender, sexuality, and anatomy, and work with allies on strategies to end those policies. There are many policies and regulations in place that impact a variety of different lives, based purely on those people's identities, and it is vital that we treat these injustices as an attack on us all. An example would be the so-called bathroom bills that gained wide popularity between 2012 and 2017, which were set to require people to use the public restrooms that corresponded to the gender they were assigned at birth. These bills target transgender people mostly, as was their aim, and their impact was disproportionately felt by them, but they obviously impacted intersex people, too, in equally unjust ways. Using fear of transgender people to provoke support for conservative politicians is an egregious affront to basic human decency. The success of these bills is indicative of the wide anxiety many people have about things they do not understand.

Conclusion

We have made a lot of enemies in our mission to end these surgeries, and we expect to make more before we finally put an end to them. But we have made a lot of friends as well. We have met people who have suffered at the hands of doctors who had sworn to protect them, and they have shared with us the importance of our goals. Our experience has been similar to that of thousands of other parents, who found themselves ripped suddenly from the bliss of the delivery room, and dropped into a scary world where all of their expectations were upended, and they had no idea what was going to happen next. Unlike most parents of intersex children, and luckily for Rosie, we were prepared for the situation. We did the research, we pushed back, we stayed patient and calm, and we stood firm. Rosie is thriving as a result, and none of the predictions of the medical establishment have come to pass.

Every day, more and more people resist these surgeries, more and more doctors begin questioning their model of care, and as a result more and more children are spared. But more can be done. And if it is true that the tide is turning against these surgeries, we may find ourselves soon facing a new problem, which is how to raise intersex children in a world where cosmetic surgery happens only after they are old enough to consent. That, we are happy to say, would be a welcome problem, one that intersex children will thank you for.

RESOURCES

Further academic reading

Davis, G. (2015) *Contesting Intersex: The Dubious Diagnosis*. New York: NYU Press.

Knight, K. and Tamar-Mattis, S. (2017) "A Changing Medical Paradigm: US Medical Provider Discomfort with Intersex Care Practices." Human Rights Watch and interACT. October 26, 2017.

Knight, K. and Tamar-Mattis, S. (2017) "'I Want to be Like Nature Made Me': Medically Unnecessary Surgery on Intersex Children in the US.' Human Rights Watch and interACT. July 25, 2017. Accessed 22 March, 2018 at https://www.hrw.org/report/2017/07/25/i-want-be-nature-made-me/medically-unnecessary-surgeries-intersex-children-us.

Murphy, T.F. (1997) *Gay Science: The Ethics of Sexual Orientation Research*. New York: Columbia University Press.

Pagonis, P. (2017) "First do harm: How intersex kids are hurt by those who have taken the Hippocratic Oath." *Griffith Journal of Law & Human Dignity 5*, 1, 40–51.

Zieselman, K. (2015) "Invisible harm." *Narrative Inquiry in Bioethics 5*, 2, 122–125.

Non-academic reading, films, and other media

Bricker, N.C. (2017) "The Intersex Rights Movement is Ready for its Moment." *The Washington Post.* October 5, 2017.

Gale, P. and Soomekh, L. (2000) *XXXY.* Stanford University Studio. (An award-winning short documentary film.)

Gregorio, I.W. (2015) *None of the Above.* London: HarperCollins. (This is an award-winning young-adult novel that deals with intersex issues.)

"I'm intersex, and it's way more common than you think." *Teen Vogue.* July 2, 2017.

Lahood, G. (2012) *Intersexion: A Documentary About Being Intersex.*

Pagonis, P. (2017) *The Son I Never Had: Growing Up Intersex.* (Autobiographical documentary film.)

Viloria, H. (2017) *Born Both: An Intersex Life.* London: Hachette Books.

The Interface Video Project. www.interfaceproject.org (Video stories of intersex people, describing their struggles.)

National Geographic (2016) *Gender Revolution: A Journey with Katie Couric*. Katie Couric explores our evolving understanding of gender identity with transgender and intersex individuals about their experiences.

Intersex support and advocacy groups

AIS-DSD Support Group. www.aisdsd.org

Human Rights Watch. www.hrw.org

interACT: Advocates for Intersex Youth. www.interactadvocates.org

Intersex Awareness Day. www.intersexday.org.

Intersex Campaign for Equality. www.intersexequality.com

Organization Intersex International (Australia). www.oii.org/au

Organization Intersex International (Europe). www.oiieurope.org

Legal assistance for intersex people

American Civil Liberties Union. www.aclu.org

interACT: Advocates for Intersex Youth. www.interactadvocates.org

Lambda Legal. www.lambdalegal.org

Southern Poverty Law Center. www.splcenter.org

NOTES

Introduction

1. Fausto-Sterling, A. (2000) *Sexing the Body: Gender Politics and the Construction of Sexuality.* Cambridge: Perseus Books.

2. *Ibid.*, p.57.

3. Kessler, S.J. (1998) *Lessons from the Intersexed.* New Brunswick: Rutgers University Press, p.12.

4. Davis, G. (2015) *Contesting Intersex: The Dubious Diagnosis.* New York: NYU Press.

5. Wang, L.C. and Poppas, D.P. (2016) "Surgical outcomes and complications of reconstructive surgery in the female congenital adrenal hyperplasia patient: What every endocrinologist should know." *Journal of Steroid Biochemistry and Molecular Biology 165,* 137–144.

6. Nokoff, N. *et al.* (2017) "Prospective assessment of cosmesis before and after genital surgery." *Journal of Pediatric Urology 13*, 1, 28e1–8e6.

7. Ellens, R. *et al.* (2017) "Psychological adjustment in parents of children born with atypical genitalia one year after their child undergoes genitoplasty." *The Journal of Urology*, May 11, 2017.

8. Knight, K. and Tamar-Mattis, S. (2017) "'I Want to be Like Nature Made Me': Medically Unnecessary Surgery on Intersex Children in the US.' Human Rights Watch and interACT. July 25, 2017. Accessed 22 March, 2018 at https://www.hrw.org/report/2017/07/25/i-want-be-nature-made-me/medically-unnecessary-surgeries-intersex-children-us.

9. Kirkland, F. (2017) "Great Ormond Street Hospital 'Failing' Intersex Children." BBC News. Accessed October 12, 2017 at www.bbc.com/news/uk-41593914.

10. Monro, S. *et al.* (2017) "Intersex, Variations of Sex Characteristics, and DSD: The Need for Change." Research Report. University of Huddersfield.

11. Diamond, M. and Sigmundson, H.K. (1997) "Sex reassignment at birth: Long-term review and clinical implications." *Archives of Pediatrics and Adolescent Medicine 151*, 3, 298–304.

12. United Nations Human Rights Council (2013) "Report of the Special Rapporteur on Torture and Other Cruel, Inhuman or Degrading Treatment or Punishment, Juan E. Méndez." February 1, 2013.

13. OHCHR *et al.* (2014) "Eliminating Forced, Coercive and Otherwise Involuntary Sterilization: An Interagency Statement." Geneva: World Health Organization. May 2014.

14. Palm Center (2017) "Re-thinking genital surgeries on intersex infants." Accessed December 9, 2017 at www.palmcenter.org/wp-content/uploads/2017/06/Re-Thinking-Genital-Surgeries-1.pdf.

15. American Medical Association (2016) "American Medical Association House of Delegates (I-16), Report of Reference Committee on Amendments to Constitution and Bylaws."

16. Creighton, S. *et al.* (2012) "Timing and nature of reconstructive surgery for disorders of sex development." *Journal of Pediatric Urology 8*, 6, 602–610.

17. The American Academy of Pediatrics (2000) "Evaluation of the newborn with developmental anomalies of the external genitalia." *Pediatrics 106*, 1, 138–142.

18. InterACT—formerly Advocates for Informed Choice; the AIS-DSD Support Group; Organization of Intersex International, which has chapters globally, to name just a few.

Chapter 1

1. Thomas, K. (2008) "Gender Tests for Olympians." *The New York Times.* July 20, 2008. Accessed February 15, 2018 at www.nytimes.com/2008/07/30/sports/30iht-GENDER.1.14880817.html.

Chapter 2

1. Hughes, I.A. *et al.* (2006) "Consensus statement on management of intersex disorders." *Archives of Disease in Childhood 91*, 7, 554–563.

2. While we prefer the term intersex, and feel that DSD is predicated on the mistaken belief that intersex children have something wrong

with them, that they have some disorder that must be treated, we understand that some people do prefer the term DSD.

3. Hughes *et al.* (2006), p.151.

4. *Ibid.*, p.159.

5. Ford, K.-K. (2001) "'First, do no harm': The fiction of legal parental consent to genital-normalizing surgery on intersexed infants." *Yale Law and Policy Review 19*, 482.

Chapter 3

1. The American Academy of Pediatrics (2000) "Evaluation of the newborn with developmental anomalies of the external genitalia." *Pediatrics 106*, 1.

2. US Food and Drug Administration (2017) "FDA Drug Safety Communication: FDA Approves Label Changes for use of General Anesthetic and Sedation Drugs in Young Children." Accessed April 27, 2017 at https://www.fda.gov/Drugs/DrugSafety/ucm554634.htm.

3. Slijper, F.M. *et al.* (1998) "Long-term psychological evaluation of intersex children." *Archives of Sexual Behavior 27*, 2, 125–144.

4. Wang, L.C. and Poppas, D.P. (2017) "Surgical outcomes and complications of reconstructive surgery in the female congenital adrenal hyperplasia patient: What every endocrinologist should know." *The Journal of Steroid Biochemistry and Molecular Biology 165*, 137–144.

5. *Ibid.*

6. Meyer-Bahlburg, H.F. *et al.* (2008) "Sexual orientation in women with classical or non-classical congenital adrenal hyperplasia as a function of degree of prenatal androgen excess." *Archives of Sexual Behavior 37*, 1, 85–99.

7. American College of Obstetricians and Gynecologists Committee Opinion Number 686. Issued January 2017. https://www.acog.org/Resources-And-Publications/Committee-Opinions/Committee-on-Adolescent-Health-Care/Breast-and-Labial-Surgery-in-Adolescents.

8. Reported in Horowitz, S. (1995) "The middle sex." *SF Weekly 13*, 5, 12.

9. Conners-Burrow, N.A. *et al.* (2009) "Adults matter: Protecting children from the negative impacts of bullying." *Psychology in the Schools 46*, 7, 593–604.

10. Preves, S.E. (2003) *Intersex and Identity: The Contested Self.* New Brunswick: Rutgers University Press, p.62.

11. *Ibid.,* p.63.

12. Crouch, N.S. *et al.* (2004) "Genital sensation after feminizing genitoplasty for congenital adrenal hyperplasia: A pilot study." *BJU International 93*, 1, 135–138.

13. *Ibid.,* p.138.

14. Creighton, S. and Minto, C. (2001) "Managing intersex: Most vaginal surgery in childhood should be deferred." *BMJ 323*, 7324, 1264.

15. Wang, L.C. and Poppas, D.P. (2017) "Surgical outcomes and complications of reconstructive surgery in the female congenital adrenal hyperplasia patient: What every endocrinologist should know." *The Journal of Steroid Biochemistry and Molecular Biology 165*, 137–144.

16. Nabhan, Z.M. *et al.* "Urinary tract infections in children with congenital adrenal hyperplasia." *Journal of Pediatric Endocrinology and Metabolism 19*, 6, 815–820.

17. Patagonis, Pidgeon (2017). Talk at the screening of *The Son I Never Had: Growing Up Intersex*. University of Wisconsin-Milwaukee, 30 November 2017.

18. Döhnert, U. *et al.* (2017) "Gonadectomy in complete androgen insensitivity syndrome: Why and when." *Sexual Development 11*, 4 , 171–174.

19. Saslow, D. *et al.* (2007) "American Cancer Society guidelines for breast screening with MRI as an adjunct to mammography." *CA: A Cancer Journal for Clinicians 57*, 2, 75–89.

20. American Society for Plastic Surgeons. "Briefing Paper: Plastic Surgery for Teenagers." Accessed February 27, 2018 at https://www.plasticsurgery.org/news/briefing-papers/briefing-paper-plastic-surgery-for-teenagers.

21. Statement by United Nations and Regional Bodies, November 2016. http://intersexday.org/en/statement-united-nations-regions.

22. Knight, K. and Tamar-Mattis, S. (2017) "'I Want to be Like Nature Made Me': Medically Unnecessary Surgery on Intersex Children in the US.' Human Rights Watch and interACT. July 25, 2017. Accessed 22 March, 2018 at https://www.hrw.org/report/2017/07/25/i-want-be-nature-made-me/medically-unnecessary-surgeries-intersex-children-us.

23. Engber, D. (2016) "Should Caster Semenya be allowed to compete against women?" *Slate.* Accessed February 18, 2018 at www.slate.com/articles/sports/fivering_circus/2016/08/should_caster_semenya_be_allowed_to_compete_against_women.

24. Butler, J. (1990) *Gender Trouble: Feminism and the Subversion of Identity.* New York: Routledge.

25. Parker, K. and Livingston, G. (2017) "6 facts about American fathers." *Pew Research Center.* Accessed February 18, 2018 at www.pewresearch.org/fact-tank/2017/06/15/fathers-day-facts.

Chapter 4

1. Knight, K. and Tamar-Mattis, S. (2017) "'I Want to be Like Nature Made Me': Medically Unnecessary Surgery on Intersex Children in the US.' Human Rights Watch and interACT. July 25, 2017. Accessed 22 March, 2018 at https://www.hrw.org/report/2017/07/25/i-want-be-nature-made-me/medically-unnecessary-surgeries-intersex-children-us.

2. Their Time: After generations in the shadow, the intersex rights movement has a message for the world: we aren't disordered and we aren't ashamed. Nora Caplan-Bricker (2017) Washington Post.

3. See *ibid.*

Chapter 5

1. Physicians for Human Rights (2017) "Unnecessary Surgery on Intersex Children Must Stop." Accessed November 10, 2017 at http://physiciansforhumanrights.org/press/press-releases/intersex-surgery-must-stop.html?referrer=https://www.google.com/?referrer=http://glma.org/index.cfm?fuseaction=Feature.showFeature&FeatureID=827&nodeID=1.

2. North American Society for Pediatric and Adolescent Gynecology (2017) "NASPAG Position Statement on Surgical Management of DSD." Accessed November 10, 2017 at http://c.ymcdn.com/sites/www.naspag.org/resource/resmgr/pdf's/NASPAG_Statement_on_DSD_PES_.pdf.

3. American Medical Student Association (2017) "AMSA Issues Statement to Defer Gender 'Normalizing' Surgeries for Children Born as Intersex." Accessed November 10, 2017 at www.amsa.

org/about/amsa-press-room/amsa-issues-statement-defer-gender-normalizing-surgeries-children-born-intersex.

4. Societies for Pediatric Urology (2017) "Physicians Recommend Individualized, Multi-Disciplinary Care for Children Born 'Intersex'." Accessed November 22, 2017 at www.spuonline.org/HRW-interACT-physicians-review.

5. US State Department (2017) "In Recognition of Intersex Awareness Day." Accessed November 10, 2017 at www.state.gov/r/pa/prs/ps/2017/10/275098.htm.

6. Strangio, C. (2017) "Stop Performing Nonconsensual, Medically Unnecessary Surgeries on Young Intersex Children." *ACLU.* Accessed November 10, 2017 at www.aclu.org/blog/lgbt-rights/stop-performing-nonconsensual-medically-unnecessary-surgeries-young-intersex.

7. The World Professional Association for Transgender Health (2017) "Standards of Care for the Health of Transsexual, Transgender, and Gender Nonconforming People. 7th Edition." Accessed November 22, 2017 at https://s3.amazonaws.com/amo_hub_content/Association140/files/Standards%20of%20Care%20V7%20-%202011%20WPATH%20(2)(1).pdf.

8. *Ibid,* p.18